Awaken Your
Creative Spirit

Capitalize On the
Divine Power Within

KEVIN HUNTER

WARRIOR
OF LIGHT
PRESS
Los Angeles, California

Warrior of Light Press
www.kevin-hunter.com

Body, Mind & Spirit/Spiritualism
Inspiration & Personal Growth

All rights reserved. Copyright ©2016
ISBN-10: 069262211X
ISBN-13: 978-0692622117

Acknowledgements

Nothing is ever permanent. Everything is temporary.
Thank you Archangel Gabriel and my Spirit team of
Guides and Angels: Luke, Veronica, Matthew, Enoch,
Jacob, Samuel, Jeremiah and Saint Nathaniel.

CHAPTERS

Introduction

I often pay attention to others concerns in their life as it assists me in addressing those issues in a book at a later date. This is especially the case if it's a common issue. This way the information is available and accessible for anyone who chooses to seek it out for eons to come. When I say *we*, I'm referring to my Spirit team of Guides and Angels in Heaven and I. The messages and guidance they filter through me come in primarily through my Clairaudience and Claircognizance channels. I'm the conduit in translating what they're giving me to share with others in a book.

Awaken Your Creative Spirit is the follow up book to *Ignite Your Inner Life Force*. Both can be read as standalone books, so have no fear if you have not read the Ignite book. First you ignite your inner life force, then you awaken your creative spirit. The creative spirit is another beautiful layer of all that you are. The life force is your true essence. You bring back your life force when you experience feelings of joy, love, and passion for something that reminds you of who your soul truly is. The joy, love, and passion high experienced is the space you create from and express yourself outwardly.

My Spirit team and I pass along some of the basics that have helped me along my often rocky and tumultuous journey. This is in order to assist you on your own path, whether you're new to the genre or you enjoy picking up on different points of view.

This book is infused with practical messages, guidance and answers that my Spirit team has taught and shared with me to pass along to those guided to my work. The main goal is to assist you in fine tuning your body, mind, and soul in order to expand your life and improve humanity one person at a time. You are a Divine communicator and perfectly adjusted and capable of receiving messages from Heaven. This is for your benefit in order to help you live a happier, richer life. It is your individual responsibility to respect yourself and this planet while on your journey here. It does not matter who you are or what your interests are. You are loved regardless if others have told you otherwise.

The messages and information enclosed in this book may be in my own words, but they do not come from me. They come from God, the Holy Spirit, my Spirit team of guides, angels and sometimes certain Archangels and Saints. I am merely the liaison or messenger in delivering and interpreting the intentions of what they wish to communicate. Often the information is a reminder for myself as well too!

I am one with the Holy Spirit and have many Spirit Guides and Angels around me. As my connections to the other side grew to be daily over the course of my life, more of them joined in behind the others. I have seen, sensed, heard and been privy to the dozens of magnificent lights that crowd around me on occasion.

If I use the word "He" when pertaining to God, this does not mean that I am advocating that he is a male. Simply replace the word, "He" with one you are comfortable using to identify God for you to be. This goes for any gender I use as examples. When I say, "spirit team", I am referring to a team of 'Guides and Angels'. The purpose of this book is to empower and help you improve yourself, your life and humanity as a whole. It does not matter if you are a beginner or well versed in the subject matter. There may be something that reminds you of something you already know or something that you were unaware of. We all have much to share with one another, as we are all one in the end. This book contains information to help you reach the place where you can be a fine tuned instrument to receive your own messages from your own Spirit team.

Some of my personal stories may be infused and sprinkled in this book. This is in order for you to see how it works effectively for me. With some of my methods, I hope that you gain insight, knowledge or inspiration. It may prompt you to recall incidents where you were receiving heavenly messages in your own life. There are helpful ways that can improve your existence and have a stronger connection with God and Heaven throughout this book. Doing so will greatly transform yourself in ways that allow you to attract wonderful circumstances at higher levels and live a happier more content life.

~Kevin Hunter

Awaken Your Creative Spirit

Capitalize On the Divine Power Within

Chapter One

Awakening the True You

*Y*our creative spirit is present when you experience positive energy flowing through you. This energy is ignited when you make a direct connection with *God*. This vibration state is where you have access to the true you, which is your higher self. Your higher self rules when you work to strip, reduce, or dissolve any negative tampering influenced by a domination of your physical surroundings. Make a connection with something greater than yourself and allow that energy Light to permeate your soul and cleanse it of toxic debris. This will assist in the process of awakening your creative spirit from slumber.

Your creative spirit is more than being artistic and getting involved in creativity pursuits, although this is a good part of it. When your creative spirit is activated by a high vibration state of being, then this is the space you create from. You can apply this to your dealings in life, your creative and artistic endeavors, and to having a greater communication line with your Spirit team on the Other Side. Your creative spirit brings your soul into a high vibration state of being because coming from a place of creativity raises your vibration.

This is the zone where you create and manifest your visions at higher levels from, while simultaneously moving you into the joy of your life. It is thinking like a kid, unleashing your inner artist, and realizing your soul's potential. When you claim your celestial power with the assistance of your heavenly helpers by your side on your Earthly life, then this assists in capitalizing the true divine power within you. *Awaken Your Creative Spirit* is an overview of what it means to have access to Divine assistance and how that plays a part in arousing the muse within you in order to bring your state of mind into a happier space.

When your soul enters its Earthly life in a human body, you are not born alone. You are accompanied by one Spirit Guide and one Guardian Angel. They are your "Spirit Team" who will remain by your side at all times from birth until you cross back over in human death. The goal they have with you is to ensure you stay on the right path that benefits your higher self. When you pay attention to their nudges, guidance, and messages, then the happier and more content your life is. When you do not follow their guidance, or take notice of when they are helping, then your life becomes chaotic, stressful, or anxiety ridden. If you are someone who works with Heaven, angels, God, archangels, ascended masters, or the Other Side regularly, then you will attract more guides and spirit Light energy sources into your vicinity that desire to help you. Some of them enter your aura to bask in your own souls light, which is like a warm sun on a gorgeous Spring day.

There are additional Heavenly helpers that may come into your life during key transitional periods in your life when it's most needed. This can be from a project you're working on that will be of benefit to you or others. They will also be present to ease your mind and heart during times of grieving and sadness. The grieving can be over the death of someone close to you, from a broken love relationship or during periods of depression. Once the additional guides or angels outside of your team have accomplished a particular quest with you, they leave to assist others, or go where they are guided to or needed. All in Heaven desire to serve because they either have no ego or very little ego. When you use the dark side of your ego, then you do not care about others. When the ego shows that it cares, it is masking an ulterior motive, or is interested in personal gain.

You are born psychic and in tune to all that is beyond the physical world. This is the natural state of your soul. You are also born operating with high vibration qualities such as love, joy, and peace. All of this begins to fade in varying degrees due to human tampering and distractions during adolescence and your developmental years. Your surroundings contain your caregivers, peers, the media you watch, and the community you reside in. All of this influences you on how to think, and what to follow, or what to believe in.

When you visit certain places around the world you'll notice that those who live in that specific community are all mostly similar to one another. They follow the same religion, or vote for the same political candidates. They have similar rituals, opinions, and belief systems, etc. There might be some minor differences, but for the most part they behave quite the same as one other. They are clones, or going along with everyone else in order to not rock the boat, to fit in, or be accepted.

There are those who reside in these communities that the majority considers to be the oddball, weird, or different. These are the ones that the community considers to be unusual from the rest of them. They are unable to hide who they truly are and reach a point of defying that if they hadn't from the beginning. They are the ones who are incredibly special and destined for greatness. Unable to suppress their creative spirit, they're also usually the ones able to access the Other Side more easily.

It takes great strength to see, feel, think, and do things differently than those around you. Think for yourself even if it defies what society or the community around you considers normal. Normalcy is a guideline that one's community insisted upon with one another, but it doesn't necessarily mean they're right. What is considered the norm is not always the case from the point of view of Spirit. It's just what the human community you are surrounded by trained you to believe.

The human mind has a great capacity for awesomeness, but the lower part of the human mind will follow anyone dangling a carrot in front of it. Your surroundings and the media tell you how to think, act, and who to lynch, or who to support. Human souls move like herds following someone they believe to be a good shepherd, or whoever their peers are raving about, or whatever fads happen to be in at that time in history. They are easily influenced and swayed within their community instead of doing the real work and research to find the highest truth for their soul.

The lone wolf who turns away from the crowd and walks in the other direction is a leader or guide in the making. They view things differently than the majority around them do, and more often than not have incarnated from a realm on the Other Side. They incarnated for a specific purpose that prompts others to view things in a broader way that eventually influences others to follow or learn from. This is for the purpose of their soul's growth. They can be someone who conveys compassion to all no matter what, even when the lynch mob around them is attacking or bullying someone else in any form.

The surroundings you grow up around can wreak havoc on your soul's inner core built system during your developmental years. This is carried on your soul's back indefinitely until it begins the laborious process of stripping away negative habits and values that were learned. This toxicity gives rise to the darker part of your ego or lower self. Your ego will do what it can to sabotage you. It can be greatly convincing that it's as if you've been taken over by the Devil himself.

The real Devil that exists in the Earth plane is the dark side of the human ego. It brings out your lower self who views circumstances and others through a bleak, toxic, and often dangerous view. They can be the bully harassing and calling others derogatory names all over the media or Internet. The ego convinces them that what they're saying is of truth, when in fact it is harmful and destructive. It helps no one around including the one dishing the harmful words, since it lowers that person's vibration as well. It's a waste of unnecessary energy that blocks good things from entering that person's life, and instead invites in more negativity. This is energy that stunts your creative spirit and dims up the communication line with your Spirit team.

Your inner light operates out of a high vibration. You have access to it since it never leaves you. When your vibration drops, then your ego and lower self rise up simultaneously. This is followed by a weakening of your inner light to the level of a pilot light waiting to be re-ignited. When it is re-ignited, the light begins to grow and fills up your soul by pushing your higher self back to the forefront of your life. The bigger the flame, the more light it attracts in, and the more in tune, and all knowing you become. This light is the doorway to God *(Spirit, Light, Essence, Power, All Knowing, the Creator, Energy, etc.)*. It is where the helpful guidance and messages come in from spirit to help you along your path. It is what assists you in attracting in your desires pending that it is aligned with your higher self's goal.

Having confidence in YOU is having confidence in God. The best parts of you are what God is. He is not a man with a beard sitting high up on a throne looking for ways to judge you. The ego is what judges others negatively. God is made up of energy that has the highest vibration traits imaginable. He is made up of love, joy, peace, confidence, optimism, forgiveness, and grace. Because His vibration is so high to the point that it's not comprehensible, this makes it difficult for human souls to reach Him. You cannot reach him when exuding any measure of negative emotion.

One of God's gifts to human souls are the Archangels and angels. They are His hands and arms assisting and guiding you to raise your vibration so that you will better be able to hear God. When you connect or communicate with an Archangel or angel, you are connecting with God. You are not praying to the angels, since they are a part of Him. When your vibration is low, then your connection to God is cut off. The angels and archangels help you to reach Him.

There are those who preach about God and Heaven in a negative, hate filled, prejudicial way with vengeful angry words that attack other people. They are not communicating with God, since there are no negative words uttered from Him or Heaven. Those words come from the dark side of human ego. The darkness of ego separates the good that exists in humanity and instead creates labels to ensure all souls are estranged from one another. All human souls are siblings of each other, since they were birthed out of the one source.

Others have been turning their backs on any mention of the word God because of the stigma that misguided souls have preached. They insist that God disapproves of you, which could not be further from the truth. His immense love for you is unconditional. He only expects that you put in an effort to be a better more compassionate person. Evolve your soul in order to move onto brighter destinies. This isn't any different than what a good parent desires for their child.

The Earth plane is a place for all student souls, whether they are here for the first time since they sparked out of God, or if they are experiencing a repeat life in order to continue their soul's education so they can continue to expand and evolve. They cannot move on until individual soul lessons are learned, gained, and accepted.   The student souls are called, *Baby Souls*. They are more naïve and innocent, yet some of them are filled with hate and destruction because they have not mastered the ego. The ego became this way due to how they were raised in their environment. Hate and negativity are passed down into the human child. When you train your child early on to have love and compassion for all souls, then they will grow up this way.

Baby souls are easy to spot as you can sense a low vibration within them that seems to be permanent, but in reality it is temporary. The vibration is stuck at that level until the soul awakens its consciousness. Until then, it is unable to expand, but instead stays exactly where it is swimming around in hatred and negativity. Some of them are also cruel, insulting, or power hungry. They are driven to put others down whether through domination or by bullying. You likely have an image of who someone like this is unless you've been cut off from all media sources and people.

There are teacher souls who incarnate from the various realms in Heaven.   Many of them are considered Wise Ones, because they seem to know all or have a "know-it-all" impression about them. They are the souls whipping the planet and its people into shape.   They have a huge ego that is revealed sporadically, but this ego leans towards correcting bad behavior or poor etiquette. Threatened souls tend to feel as if they're being lectured by the Wise One. This is the Wise Ones nature at their core as they have a dominating cold and at times aggressive air about them.

Some of the other teacher souls are called, Incarnated Elementals. They make up a great deal of the activists around the world contributing positive change to anything associated with the environment, animals, plants, the oceans, and all of nature. They have a stronger ego than the Wise One that can become aggravated when feelings of insecurity rise or when someone has caused harm to any of the Elemental's fights.

There are also the Star People (*a.k.a. Star Seed, Star Child, Star Soul*) who are the quiet hardworking ones implementing incredible technological inventions to assist the planet in progressing. They use much less ego than the Elementals and Wise Ones. This has helped them to stay focused on creating in the technological world. They don't use or show much emotion and tend to be on an even keel. Through spirit assistance, they came up with the computers, cars, and anything technologically manmade, but helpful devices. While these inventions have caused problems and contributed to blocking souls from picking up on heavenly messages to assist their life, it has also helped them in many positive ways. How would you get to work quickly without transportation? Now you can have an email pen pal with someone on the other side of the world. Social media online has helped bring people together, but it has also torn them apart at the same time. This is because the dark side of human ego has abused the inventions given to them. It's like a naughty child throwing a toy across their room in a tantrum because they didn't get their way. My team has always called that *the noise*, because that is all it is.

There are the Incarnated Angels, who are the compassionate highly sensitive souls that feel the most heaviness from human cruelty, but they bring love and compassion to those without it. They get others who are blind to love to notice that you can accomplish great things and get your point across without being nasty.

These are a few examples of how to recognize who is an evolved teacher soul that has agreed to incarnate into a human body for purposes that benefit others. All of them contribute to slapping the baby souls away who behave badly or disrespectfully.

Children and animals have the highest ranges of psychic abilities than any other being on Earth. Children haven't been fully tampered with and destroyed by jaded adults. When a child is scared or explains that they're seeing something no one else is, an adult automatically tells them, "Oh, it's just your imagination." There isn't a worse phrase to tell a child who is confiding in you about something that may be present that a cynical adult no longer understands. This phrase is what begins the process of erecting blocks to divine communication in that child's life. In all fairness, it's not the adults fault entirely. They are a product of the environment they were raised in. They we're trained to view things that are not understood by the ego to be a figment of one's imagination. Be open minded to what a child is telling you. They see, hear, feel, and know far more than adults give them credit for.

Animals remain as the spirit beings whose psychic range stays relatively the same throughout the course of its life. It doesn't have the kinds of blocks that human souls create. An animal isn't concerned with paying rent or a mortgage. It's not concerned about finding work or stressing out over triviality. As long as it's fed, has a place to sleep, and with an owner who loves it, then there are little blocks in its world if any at all.

Imagination is the source where your creative spirit is awakened. This space is the portal that leads to a stronger communication line with Heaven. The artists of the world and throughout history have greater access to the Divine because they have a good degree of sensitivity and imagination. They can walk through another's shoes without judgment, no matter horrible that other person might be. Gifted actors excel at this as well. This open mindedness is one of the keys to having a crystal clear connection line with your Spirit team.

It's not uncommon for super young people who have strong connections with the other side to have fear wondering who is around them or why. Sometimes those who appear for them are Guides or Angels, and other times they are spirits who have not crossed over into the light and are unaware that they've gone. They're stuck in the transition between the Earth and spiritual plane. Spirits are attracted to the Light whether already on the other side or in this plane.

Children and animals have larger lights around them than adults because they haven't been stripped of this light due to blocks created in the physical world. This is why the spirit has a tendency to gravitate and surround them. They can't cause harm and are not trying to. They're attracted to the light and the life force of the human soul. It's like being attracted to anything where you want to get close and feel it. Some young people are so fearful of it that overtime as they grow older the connection and light dims. As a result, they refuse to acknowledge it as an adult.

Chapter Two

Spirit Is In Your Corner

There is a free will law that says no spirit being can intervene with any soul to make choices and decisions for them, unless that soul has specifically requested it. This means when you desire something or you need help with anything, you send out a request to Heaven. This can be done in prayer, mentally, in writing, or out loud. If you do not ask, then they are not allowed to intervene in your life unless it is to prevent a life endangering situation that might result in death before your time. Other than that, you're on your own until you ask for help. Your Spirit team will guide and nudge you along your path, but unless you're paying attention to these cues there is little they can do.

You can call upon whoever you're comfortable with communicating to, such as God, Heaven, your Spirit Guide, Guardian Angel, departed loved one, Archangel, Saint, or Ascended Master. You can do this at anytime or any hour of the day. Heaven understands what you desire in your heart, but they need to hear you make the formal request. I've mentioned in the past that it's much like the mythological image of the

Vampire, where they cannot enter your house without an expressed invitation from you. This is similar in how Spirit beings in Heaven work. You need to invite them into your life if you want them working with you.

It doesn't matter how you ask, but that you do ask. You can say something like, "Please help me find another job." Discuss the kind of job you desire, but avoid laying out how you want something to come about. Leave the *how* and *when* up to them. They will orchestrate what needs to happen when the timing is right. This is pending that it is aligned with your higher self's goal. Your higher self uses the least amount of ego. While your ego might desire something, your higher self isn't interested in triviality or superficiality. Have faith and a strong belief that Heaven is in your corner, even if it feels like there is a long delay or stagnancy period going on before results appear to be forthcoming.

When I was sixteen, I knew that I was going to write books one day. I wanted to write and no one was going to stop me in working at my passion and purpose. I knew I had to get a regular job first. I had a strong connection with my team of guides and angels when I was a child and beyond. From adolescence, I had been working with them, communicating with them, and following their guidance. I asked my team for help with getting this first job at a record store. This was back when record stores existed. My team guided me in steps to make that happen.

I wanted to get into the film business not long after that, so I asked my team for help with that. I followed their guidance in trying to get in. To give you some perspective, it was weeks after my twenty-third birthday when I got my foot in the door of the entertainment business. This was by joining a major A-list Hollywood actress as her film development guy. This entailed reading scripts submitted to her and writing coverage on it. All great things came down from that point. You'll note that it took about six years for something like that to happen, but it did end up happening in an even bigger way than I expected. This is an example of Heaven intervention and assistance. When I asked for help, it eventually came to light. When I did nothing, then that was exactly what I got. I've been testing them out my entire life through trial and error. This has helped me discover how they work.

When you ask for help, guidance, or intervention, then step out of the way and allow the assistance to come about. Release and let go of the need to push for an answer or the need to control a situation. When you call up a friend you don't repeat the same phrases as if they didn't hear you the first time. You say it once and then move onto something else.

You can repeatedly request something to your Spirit team, but it will only make you grow aggravated and frustrated when you receive nothing right away. Days pass and you're feeling miserable wondering. "I don't get it. I've been praying and repeatedly asking for help with this, but nothing is coming. Maybe this isn't real or they're ignoring me."

Those in Heaven view circumstances on Earth from a different perspective. They do not get caught up in the human ego drama and tantrums that we sometimes fall into. If you feel you're being ignored, then it's likely your ego having a fit, which Heaven is indifferent to. They are not fazed or affected by ego spectacle the way we can sometimes be.

All of the stuff in the media, human politics, and people arguing with one another is seen as triviality and a waste of time and energy from the perspective of those in Heaven. Being caught up in that space is what can cause a long delay of inactivity until you step away from being completely absorbed in pettiness.

What Heaven pays attention to is someone who has a huge growing light around them. This is someone who is contributing to humanity in a positive way. It is someone who is doing their best to be a compassionate loving person. Those are the ones that widen the eyes of a high vibration spirit in Heaven. They want to help that soul, but sometimes they have to maneuver situations that require another person to pay attention.

For instance, you want a job at a specific company. You've put in a request for help from your Spirit team, but time has passed and nothing has surfaced. If it doesn't come about, then take into consideration the possibilities that you're not privy to. One of them is that the person responsible for hiring staff is not paying attention to the guidance from their own Spirit team to bring you on. Another reason is that this job would not make you happy, even though you cannot see that right away. Your Spirit team can see how it would end if you joined that particular company. It would not end well in your favor, so they keep it from happening and continue to guide you to the place of employment they see you joining and being happier at. This concept is applied to all aspects of one's life including a desire for a loving relationship partner or a new place to move to. They might keep you away from someone you have a love crush on because they know it would not benefit your higher self. The person might be abusive in some form that would cause you prolonged heartache. Later down the line, you connect with someone out of this world that is better than the one you had the crush on.

Know that you are loved more than you can comprehend. It is the same way a parent that has several children. This is where one child is a handful stomping their feet in a dramatic irritating tantrum, and the other child is the one who is focused and on an even keel. While the parent loves both children the same, they might secretly admire the child who is together in all ways. If you were that child, and felt that this was not the case, then this is because the parent is operating from their lower self and ego. They might feel threatened, jealous, or envious that you as a child are a much greater person than they have been able to reach. There is some resentment and it bruises their ego that you are incredibly awesome.

Many of the teacher souls and those from the various realms have felt hated growing up because of the way people treated them for being different. Wise Ones have had to put up with others being threatened by them. The Wise One has an arrogant sure of themselves aura and tone about them. It almost seems as if they are looking down on others even though it's not intentional. The lower self and ego in others is threatened by confidence. What they should be doing is looking at that as an opportunity to improve their soul.

Putting a request into Heaven in prayer once a day can be sufficient enough for a desire. You will need to put in at least one request for them on a matter before they can intervene and assist. This is because they cannot interfere with your free will choice or your life without your expressed permission.

You're allowed the freedom to live your life the way you see fit pending it's not hurting yourself or someone else. You place your request with Heaven, and then you walk away. You busy yourself with other things and don't fret or think about the request you made. Let them help while you focus on something else. This is why they are called your Spirit team, because they are your team who works with you. Avoid trying to think about how the prayer will be answered, because often times it's answered in a way that you do not expect.

Sometimes ones prayers are answered immediately and other times it may be delayed for a reason. If there are life lessons you must endure in a particular circumstance, then this could be one reason for a delay. Notice or pick up on the guidance they continue to filter through you.

You find yourself saying, "I kept getting this nudge to call this person up and I continuously brushed it off. I finally called them and what I wanted came to be!" This is your Guide or Angel nudging you to make that call.

Heaven communicates to you through your etheric senses. When your senses are clear of debris, toxins, and blocks, then the clearer the messages are. This is one of the reasons they insist that everyone work on being clear minded, exercise regularly, head out into nature, take time outs, avoid negative people, and watch what you ingest into your body. Those action steps contribute to you being a fine tuned communication machine with your Spirit team. Being in nature is one of the greatest healing places to be in. The messages come in clearer in those areas.

Your Spirit team of Guides and Angels are at your disposal. Ask for help and intervention with anything you desire. Understand that there may be delays to fulfilling your request, or they might have something better in mind for you. They will also only deliver what is aligned with your higher self. Develop a daily relationship with God, Heaven, and your Guides and Angels. They cannot intervene with your free will, which is why you need to specifically request their assistance. They can help with giving you strength in a tough situation, motivating you to write that letter for the job you're interested in, or to obtain that potential love mate you have your eye on. If it appears that what you desire is not happening, then take into account the various possible reasons for that. When you are tuned into Heaven, then the reasons filter through you effortlessly. Centering yourself and getting your ego out of the way helps you to be more able to pick up on the possible explanations. This can be that what you're asking for is not aligned or beneficial to your higher self's growth and path. There are circumstances that need to be maneuvered in order to make it happen. Your Spirit team has a list of variables in the way that are challenging. This can be something such as working with someone's free will choice including your own.

Many human souls no longer pay attention or listen to their team's wisdom, let alone believe in a higher power. And even those who believe in a higher power are unaware they have a Spirit team they can connect with. They might believe the process to be associated with witchcraft or hocus-pocus. A lack of faith in your team blocks the incoming messages and guidance. Your Spirit team is relaying action steps you need to take through their guidance, but you're ignoring those steps, or brushing it off due to assuming it is wishful thinking, laziness, or procrastination. Your Spirit team will continue to give you the same guidance repeatedly until you follow it. Once you do, then you're shown the next step to take and so on.

Chapter Three

Picking Up On Heavenly Input

*H*eavenly guidance can come through as a light bulb idea planted into your consciousness that causes you to leap with excitement and joy. It not only brings you pleasure, but others as well. Sometimes you make decisions that you believe to be heavenly guidance, but then you later get smacked down. It did not go as planned and you wonder if it was your ego that had pushed you to go after something instead of your Spirit team. This is where it can be tricky because you don't know if you're accurately receiving heavenly messages and guidance. Your Spirit team may guide you to go after something, but then you find you fail at it. This is not a failure in the way you equate disappointment to be. You fall down on your face after the first few tries, but you get up and climb back on that horse again. You learn more from failures than you do successes. It builds character and gives you the tools that will become valuable when achievement happens. You incorporate those lessons gained into the success that comes about at a later date.

Believe that you can do anything you want when

you go after it with passion and persistence. Develop a relationship with your Spirit team and work with them regularly as you move along your life's path. They will show you the next move you need to take in steps. First you take one step, then they show you the next one and so forth. If someone takes years to pick up on the one step that's being relayed, then it will feel as if you're not moving. Your Spirit team is waiting for you to take that one step in order to show you the next one.

Do you have trouble connecting with Heaven? Stop what you're doing, including overthinking things, and then move into a place of stillness in order to center yourself. In that state, you are better able to pick up on the heavenly input of your Guide and Angel. The act of listening is being in tune and receptive to the information, guidance, and messages being filtered through you from beyond. You can practice listening with those around you. Strike up a conversation with a friend, acquaintance, or family member. Ask them questions so that the floor belongs to them. Sit back and listen to their response absorbing the words they're saying. Care about what they're telling you.

God and your Spirit team always communicate with you. No one is exempt from that, but the question is, "Are you listening?" When you talk excessively or cannot shut off the voices of your ego, it can be impossible to pick up on what your Spirit team is trying to convey to you.

Meditating is a good place to start in order to pick up on heavenly input. This is getting into a quiet space at least once a day if you can. Turn off all distractions around you including cell phones and the television.

Close your windows briefly if you live on a street where you hear the noise of traffic, horns honking, loud talking, or sirens. If you play music, go for something ambient, chill-out, soft, or classical. Anything that is not loud and obtrusive. Adjust the volume level to one that is loud enough that it is not a distraction, or too low you can barely hear it. I love loud rock music since I am a classic rocker after all, but when I need to connect or channel, then I change my music selection to something of an ambient, soft, and etheric nature. It is also turned down to a lower level.

Shut your door if you live with others who are being rambunctious and noisy, or if they're the types that constantly interrupt you when your door is open. Sit or lie down in a comfortable position in order to be in a calm state. Spirit messages are picked up on much easier when you're in a tranquil state of mind. This is because when you're stressed, busy, or have distractions going on, then those are potential blocks that prevent one from picking up heavenly input.

It can take anywhere from five minutes or more depending on how easy or challenging it is for you to move into this calm state. When you are in this comfortable relaxed position, then there is room for God to come in.

Avoid straining to pick up on anything as that will block the input. Instead relax and allow the energy to flow through you naturally. Don't expect anything or try to push for messages or an answer. Remain in a content state where you are centered and not seeking anything out.

Ask your Spirit team to show you signs that they're around you. The signs can be meticulously subtle, but when you're in tune to all that is around you outside of the physical world, then you pick up on the symbols effortlessly and you know without a doubt that it is a message. There is no second-guessing, which comes from your ego.

Visualize a pathway out in nature that is winding through the grass up to two closed doors side by side next to one another. Watch the doors open gradually allowing in light. This light is shining onto the focus of your dreams and desires. The doors are being pushed wide open. On the other side of that door are the moving images of what you desire. This is a canvas where you can allow your imagination to go wild in painting all of the things you've ever wanted.

Work with your Spirit team by connecting with them regularly as if you would a close friend. Ask for regular guidance on the steps you need to take in order to obtain your dreams and desires. Ask Heaven for courage when you feel fear, or if you need a boost in faith when you experience doubt. Solicit for supplies or additional income to put into your dream.

The basic action steps are to pray, ask for help, listen, take action, put in positive energy and passion, and then believe it is here now. Combine those steps into a delicious cocktail of positive manifesting strength.

When you are a fine tuned well oiled machine, then the communication line with your Spirit team can be effortless. They will nudge you when it's safe to take the next step in going after what you want. They will let you know when to pull back or when to dive head on in. They see more than the human eye can fathom or comprehend. They have an airborne view of what's to come for you and they know when it's safe to proceed on. You might ask for help with something, but then it doesn't come to pass. Sometimes you have to give it time. Months go by and suddenly what you asked for surfaces or a problem you had is resolved.

Many have expressed frustration due to working so hard and contributing so much, yet they feel there isn't enough return or pay off. Maybe you're not being rewarded or compensated at all. While the work itself is its own reward, you live in a world that requires monetary compensation for basic necessities in order to survive. Have patience and keep on trucking forward. A winner perseveres regardless of setbacks, rejections, or delays. Heaven is aware of what you've been doing and they want to see you be at a place where you're at peace. Know that they cannot wave a magic wand and the monetary success you desire comes flying into your lap. They cannot force your next love partner to knock on your front door. They do what they can from where they are to help make things happen for you as long as it's aligned with your higher self's path and not ego filled desires.

They give you clues and signs while they attempt to communicate with you on what you can do to help make it happen along quicker. When you are in tune, then you are in harmony to the guidance and steps your Spirit team is filtering through you to assist you along your life's path and in conquering your dreams. Keep in mind they are also wrestling with the free will choices of those who can help you attain success.

Roadblocks can be something like you desire a love partner and your team has one in mind. The issue is that both you and this potential partner are not paying attention to Heaven. Instead you are both ruling through free will choice. One or the both of you might not be following the guidance you're being given. There is a gradual progression upwards to your dreams as you move through life by following the direction your Spirit team is aiming towards.

You might compare yourself to someone who you consider to be more successful in your field. You say, "I'm so much better than that person. Why do they have success and I have nothing when I work so much harder?"

When it comes to love you complain, "How come that person has a fantastic love partner who appreciates and adores them, when I'm so much more of a compassionate and loving person and would appreciate my partner more than they do?"

Envy is a low vibration feeling energy that hurts you. It lowers your vibration, which blocks incoming abundance and leads you to feeling frustrated. It pushes your desires further away and blocks your connection with Heaven. There is no shame for having uttering envious words, but work on catching yourself when you find you've moved into jealousy or envy. Those feelings are detrimental to you. If you are an awesome and wonderful hardworking soul, then avoid allowing negativity to enter your field. Stay focused on what you need to do and be anchored by faith and passion. Circumstances may be dormant, but nothing relatively bad is happening to you, yet you feel stuck beyond comprehension. Look at how far you've come and the progress you've made, rather than why the things you desire have not shown up yet.

Heaven and the angels save you in a myriad of ways that sometimes might seem pretty small at the time, but in hindsight appear fated. Rock singer, Alanis Morissette, has one of the best selling albums of all time called, *Jagged Little Pill*. The album came out about a week after her 21st birthday in 1995. When she was nineteen years old and moved to Los Angeles, she ran into some trouble. She was heading home carrying two bags with her. One of the bags had her money in it and the other bag had the lyrics to her not yet recorded album, *Jagged Little Pill*.

A thief was following her and came at her with a gun. She felt enormous panic and fear praying that this person would not take the bag that had her *Jagged Little Pill* lyrics. Guess which bag he took?

He took the bag with her money and not the bag that had her lyrics for *Jagged Little Pill*, an album that was bought by nearly almost everyone on the planet when it came out. It ended up selling over 33 million copies. It's been on numerous top best selling lists. At press time it is the 12th highest selling album in history.

What if the thief had taken her work instead of the money? There was a reason he was prompted to take the money instead of the art. At that time, she was broke and had not become a financially successful artist yet. The money taken was all of her funds. It was interesting that she was relieved that the money was stolen and not the lyrics.

As a creative artist, I understand how the art overtakes the money. I was working on my computer when out of a clumsy reflex I smacked my tea, which fell onto the keyboard. Within minutes the computer shut down and did not turn back on. My heart raced with panic. This was not because I would have to shelve out money for another computer, but because I had spent the week producing so much writing work that I worried it was gone for good. There is no way I could repeat it word for word. I hadn't yet transferred the work out onto a flash drive for back up as I do pretty regularly. I know this is not the same as being robbed, but the point was that the money was less of an issue over losing my work. Luckily, the computer was saved as well as my work for a very low fee much less than anticipated. I also attribute that to asking for immediate assistance and intervention by my team after the accident.

Money is a piece of paper that we apply value to. In this Alanis story, she needed money, but it wasn't of importance to her when face to face with the thief. It was the creative art she feared losing. The money came to her later by not craving it on any level. It wasn't something she sought out.

Chapter Four

The Great Outdoors

*E*very cell is made up of energy. There is no space that does not have energy in it. This energy is where God resides. The law of attraction is a universal law that says the energy you put out is what you will get in return. If you think or feel something negative, then this will be sent out into the universe and multiply. It will act as a boomerang and re-route itself and be sent right back to you. If you choose to think positive thoughts, then this will be what is re-directed back to you. There are countless books on the law of attraction topic, because so many have experienced the results whether it was negative or positive. It's not just some whimsical philosophy. Even those who have no belief in God or a higher power are hip to the laws of attraction. You can choose to be negative and live in misery, or you can find a space where cheerfulness exists.

For centuries, astrologers have been studying the scientific aspects of how the planets affect the people on Earth depending on its movement in the Heavens. This is not to be confused with the fun horoscope section listed in magazines. When there is a Full Moon, many have admitted to experiencing more inner turmoil than usual. They may feel anxious, depressed, or wrestle with insomnia. When the planet Venus moves Retrograde it tends to dissolve relationships that we're already on unstable ground to begin with, or propel them to question the connections they're currently in. Five of my past love relationships had all ended during a Venus Retrograde. This transit won't end a relationship that is rock solid. The planets don't make things happen, but just as every individual is made up of energy, so are the planets. Having an understanding of how everything around you is made up of energy gives you a broader perspective of human life. It assists you in navigating through it with more ease than you normally would.

Govern your life through positive faith, viewpoints, feelings, and thoughts. Every organism, object, and all matter that exists is made up of energy. This can be from people, to plants, to animals, to the rocks, to planets, to anything you can think of. All of this energy is what God is. You cannot escape it even if you tried, or if you chose to ignore it.

When you find yourself floundering, experiencing negative feelings, or you're attracted to addictive substances and behavior patterns, then call on Heaven and your Spirit team for support. Ask them to help guide you out of the negative space you've tumbled into. Pay attention to any guidance that is being relayed to you. You will feel it, hear it, know it, or see it.

The nudges may be to push you get outside in the great outdoors. Sometimes you'll be guided to go to the beach if you're near one, or a body of water, take a walk, or some other physical activity in nature. All in Heaven know that when you are in a nature setting that they can work on enhancing your soul more swiftly by relaxing your mind in that environment than anywhere else. They will clear away any cobwebs that have developed within and around your soul. Continue to ask for their assistance daily until you begin to notice the shifts taking place within that pull you out of any inner turmoil.

As a gifted person, you will learn to govern your lifestyle choices in different ways than someone who is not as sensitive. You will want to be extra careful with the kinds of people you surround yourself with, where you live, and the kinds of food and drinks you ingest. If any of this is negative, then it can attack your energy. This is called a *psychic attack* in some circles. Taking frequent walks or active exercise in a nature setting is always advised. This is because the spirit power is heavier wherever God's creation is. There is also some familiarity in those settings as it gives the soul a sliver of a glimpse of what it's like back home in Heaven.

Spirits do not congregate in large numbers around corporate buildings. They prefer to be among flowers, plants, trees, mountains, beaches, and grass. The Earth was made this way for a reason before human souls built concrete things on it. While that was beneficial to human survival, it soon ran wild and out of control with overdeveloping in areas that should have stopped ages ago. Just because there is a tiny bit of land left doesn't mean it should be used for a building.

If you're not near a nature setting, then do your best to visualize you are. This will help keep you centered and grounded. You absorb more stress than someone who is less sensitive. It causes anxiety when you're in situations that make you unhappy. When you're dejected, then this can push you to reach for an addictive substance to temporarily get rid of that feeling. Your imagination is a powerful friend. It can paint you pictures of places beyond. It can help in attracting or repelling that which you desire or do not want.

The period where I'm writing a book is where I am the most centered and in control. When my creative piece is finished, I fall into a little depression not knowing what to do with myself. To go from a creative high to nothing is a far place to fall. Those around me, along with my Spirit team, will urge me to get back to work since they know when I'm being creative is when I'm floating above the world. Luckily, over time and with much effort, I've managed to find ways to experience joy beyond when I'm not working on artistic creative endeavors.

You sit on a huge rock pile formation in the middle of a quiet National Park gazing at a gigantic mountain in front of you in the distance, and you can sense the uplifting energy swirling within and around you. Any stresses you were previously experiencing lift gently off your body. Your soul experiences freedom being able to reach and understand what God is. There are no tampering energies and distractions such as people or technology messing with your equilibrium. Spirit power is heavy in those areas more than any other. This is why many call these vast untouched nature settings *power places*.

Your Spirit team can reach you much easier in a

nature setting and you can pick up on their communication waves with little effort there. It's more challenging to connect when you are standing on a busy street corner with wall to wall skyscrapers, a sea of backed up cars in all directions, and people rushing past one another with a cold unfriendly vibe. There is little spirit guide and angel energy in those pockets, because they're not drawn to noise the way the ego is. They are present, but not in massive numbers the way they are in any setting that is not manmade.

There might be a few people you bump into while in a park like setting, but most of them are there for the same reasons you are. That is to escape and get away into quiet nature to re-connect with their soul, God, or something bigger that is outside of themselves. Some enjoy doing this to admire the beauty of nature itself. The human eye and spirit eye are both attracted to magnificence. This includes the brilliance that exists in someone's light as well as the splendor in nature.

Others head into a nature setting to have a deeper connection with the physical earth, which assists in grounding you. When you enter a national park for example, you're basically off the grid. Your mobile phone no longer works, or the signal is difficult to obtain. This is a forced technological detox that is beneficial to your overall well being. Put all of those distractions down for a bit to remain still and focused on something greater than the physical world. You can find a nature setting near where you live that feels as if you're off the network. You might even be lucky enough to reside in such a place so you know the daily calmness and inner peace that comes with that.

Retreating and taking regular time outs are not

only a luxury, but a necessity for your soul, mind, and body. The angels are huge advocates for human souls taking frequent breaks, time outs, vacations, and retreats. If you cannot afford vacations or long weekend trips away, then ask for regular Heavenly help to come up with the funds or an alternative. Either way, you can take time outs without going away or spending any money. You can take regular walks around the block, or head to a nature locale whether it's a park or your own backyard. Create a space in your home where you can relax and zone out allowing your mind to wander. All of this assists in giving you great ideas, awakens your creative side, and recharges your physical batteries giving you a nice lift in energy and optimism.

We sometimes hear that when people are in jail, some of them suddenly find God. You have likely heard stories of inmates suddenly reading the Bible. When everything has been stripped away from you, and your left with your own thoughts, you eventually seek out the meaning of life and what is God. You no longer have the tampering distractions of the physical world.

Examine the types of people around you, and what state or overall mood they tend to put you in. When you hang around others who are gossips and always complaining, you'll notice that it feels as if your energy spirals downhill. Suddenly you feel miserable, agitated, or moody. You we're doing incredible before you and this person had a conversation. You might immediately nod recalling someone like this in your life that fits this description. You discover you're always trying to get them off the phone or move them out of your vicinity. Choose to be around people who are joyful, objective, open minded, and optimistic.

Take note in the past when you were in a perpetual negative state, and how it felt as if it were one thing after another happening to you, then notice when you were riding on cloud nine, happy, and optimistic. Look at what that brought you in the process. All of this is energy and the way you're choosing to direct it or react to it. You throw that energy out into the universe and it creates a ricochet effect where the energy is darted right back at you. If you throw out negativity, then that's what comes back and hits you. You toss out positivity, then that's what is returned.

When there was a job I wanted, I had profound immense passion within me. There was an endless reserve of optimistic energy and belief that I would get that job. I knew without a doubt that it would happen, and as a result it did. When I doubted that a relationship would work out, I created a self-fulfilling prophecy that ultimately ended it. Over the course of my entire life, I've experimented with the law of attraction and this energy. I've watched the results of what would follow based on the vibration of my state of mind at that time.

Have gratitude with all the good you have now. Be thankful for the blessings that exist in your life at the present moment. This means not only saying that you're grateful, but feeling this appreciation as well too. Saying the words and feeling them are ingredients added to a recipe that creates abundance.

"I am grateful for having a job that pays all of my bills. I'm grateful for having a car that runs, and food and clothing, a place to live...." And so on.

When you have the things you want, one has a tendency to take it for granted until they lose those things. You get too comfortable with having the basic necessities of life handed to you.

You have at least one thing in your life that is good. Maybe it's that you have strong health or that you have a place to live. It may not be in the city, dwelling, or community you love, but you have a roof over your head and you're protected. It could be that you're living paycheck to paycheck and that stresses you out. When you pull back to look at it from a higher perspective you'll notice your rent or mortgage gets paid every month on time. Granted it might feel stressful that the bulk of the money you make goes to that, but at least you have a place to live when others are living on the streets and don't have that necessary luxury.

Saying *thank you* to your Spirit team is helpful in immense ways. How would you feel constantly doing something for a demanding child who never shows appreciation? "I need. I need. I need."

Say to God and your Spirit team that you are appreciative for what you have. Gratitude and appreciation is high vibration energy. High vibration energy attracts equally good stuff back to you. When you're negative and complaining regularly about what you don't have or how things are not going your way, then that energy expands and ensures that this cycle continues.

When you complain about where you're life is at,

take a step back and add, "But at least I have a place to live with a roof over my head. I never worry that I can't pay my rent. I am blessed in that respect."

Be appreciative for the practical necessities that you have. This is shifting negative complaining energy into something positive. What you're thinking and feeling now is what dictates the direction of how your life will go in the coming months.

Learn to use the phrase, "Thank you."

Thank your spirit team, God, or whoever you're comfortable with for providing the necessities needed to survive on this planet. Thank them when your desires come to fruition. The feeling behind being grateful is a high vibration energy which attracts in more of the same. When you find that you've been running on a tangent of negative energy, or you've succumbed to gossip, then catch yourself and shift those words and thoughts into a new higher vibration topic. Don't beat yourself up when you make a mistake. Simply correct it and shift the energy as you become aware of it.

If you find that you keep attracting in the same types of friendships and love relationships, then shift and raise your vibration. Rise to the energy level of the kind of person you want to attract in. Give the energy time to work its magic. Results vary where it might be instant, or it could take several months to come about. Shifting your vibration energy takes work, because it's not a matter of shifting one day, and then going back to who you were the next day. When you go back to who you normally are the next day, then your vibration has shifted again. Vibration energy needs to be consistent. If your attitude is consistently negative, then this is what influences your circumstances and what will enter your vicinity. Do your best to practice reverting into a state of optimism whenever you find yourself floundering.

Chapter Five

Be the Chief
Executive of Your Life

*W*ho doesn't want positive abundance flowing into their lives? Most everyone desires some level of monetary success to live on the planet comfortably without worry knowing that their bills are paid, with clothes on their back and food on the table. Money is considered evil in some circles, but that is a dramatic statement since money is only as important as the value you place on it. Abundance and success is not only related to money. It can be success in a love relationship, or victory in any accomplishment you've succeeded in. This includes inner spiritual success.

Your soul's life moves in cycles in the same way that your human life moves in phases. These cycles are full of endings and new beginnings. Your day comes to an end when you head off to sleep at whatever time that might be. When you wake up the next day, you start a new beginning. Look at this new beginning as if it is a new page within the chapter of the book you're writing that is your life. You are the manager of your existence and your soul. Direct each day in the manner that you would like it to go. Take control of this page within the chapter of your book and write the words that you want to see happen.

When you begin each day with the intention that it will be full of good, then this is far more effective than beginning your day with worry, anger, sadness, or any other negative emotion. The state of mind you choose to begin your day in is what will dictate how your day will go. Wake up each day with the objective that you will feel good. If you're heading to your job, then head into work experiencing greatness! Even if you're not a big fan of your job, it is far more effective energy having a positive mindset and making the most of it rather than shuffling in miserable. Having a positive mindset is what brightens up your day and those around you. It is also what brings more of that good stuff into your life because this energy is a magnet bringing something of equal or greater value to you. It's inevitable that there will be roadblocks that drop down in the way on your path. You could run into a toxic person or even work with one. When that happens, you will deal with it like an efficient executive since you are the CEO of your life. Allow those moments that ruin your great day to evaporate. Mentally scoop it up with your hand and toss it out like you're pitching a softball as far as it can go.

SELF FULFILLING PROPHECIES

Everyone wants to feel good about their life. Concern settles in when it's not going according to the way you dream or desire. You worry that the things you want will never happen or that you're going to be perpetually stuck. These are fear-based thoughts that come from the ego. Life is always moving and changing. Nothing stays permanently the same. Look at the decisions or the non-action choices you're making or have made that are a result of you feeling stuck. If you get up every morning to spend your day surfing the Internet up until lunchtime, then how will anything change in your life? That's an example of how non-action won't bring you the results you crave.

There are moments when non-action is an action in itself. Sometimes you're guided to not make any decisions until the coast is clear or divine timing has taken place. This is about making no choices that positively contribute to a change happening in your life.

Worry is a fear-based emotion that comes from your ego, but it is also a natural human experience. It is an emotion that creates a block between you and what you crave. It is a normal reaction to feel fear that something is not going the way you hoped. Concern comes about when something isn't going your way, or you're about to make a big change in your life. When this happens, call on your Spirit team and ask them to help give you faith, strength, support, and direction.

From the angels perspective there is nothing to be concerned about. They see that all will always be well in the end when you have Heaven in your corner. It might feel as if it's impossible not to worry about a situation while you're moving through a specific experience, but when you worry, then you create a self-fulfilling prophecy that brings more obstacles into your life that will add even more anxiety. Thoughts produce things and can magnify a situation by bringing similar situations that are equal to the emotion you're experiencing.

A common phrase said by other is, "Why do bad things keep happening to me?" When you worry about one thing, then this brings about other similar things. When you feel uneasiness about anything at all, call upon your Spirit team and request that they ease your heart and mind of this worry. Understand the concept that in the bigger picture worry never lasts since situations never last. There are peaks and valleys or highs and lows in one's life. Eventually your soul will travel back home upon your human death and then the worry is suddenly irrelevant and non-existent.

When experiencing fearfulness, not only is it effective to ask for help, but also work on changing the tone and overall essence of your emotions and thoughts to that of love. This is thinking or saying something like, "All will be well in the end. I know this without a doubt. None of this matters and this too shall pass."

When you lose your job, the emotions experienced will vary from one person to another. Some will understandably worry about how they will pay their bills, while others will adopt a newfound amazing positive energy out of the job loss. They will see it as a blessing in disguise since deep down they were terribly unhappy at this job to begin with. It was soul crushing and sucking out their life force. When the job was taken away out of nowhere, then their soul eventually experiences freedom. You are now free to start a new chapter in your life.

If you've been unhappy at your job, then look for

work that will excite you and bring out your passionate side. When something is lost, something else is gained in the end. In order to bring in a new and better situation, the universe will abruptly remove something to make room for what's to come. At first your ego will look at it in panic, while your higher self will see the potential that can come out of it.

This is the same with love relationships. When you lose someone who meant the world to you because that person decided they were no longer interested, or the connection has run its course, then you open the door to allowing someone in who is more aligned with you, your values, and who you are.

In my past work life, I've accepted job offers where I was making less than what I made in prior jobs, but in the end the money multiplied over time to the point where I was making double what I had ever made before. The reason I accepted a job that was little pay was because I eagerly wanted to do that particular work for various reasons including the knowledge I would gain from the experience. The money came in effortlessly and in bigger ways than it had ever done. This was because my vibration was high. I looked at the job with joy, love, and excitement. I wanted to be doing that kind of work. I would have done it for free. It wasn't about the money and therefore the money came rolling in as a result. Sometimes there is a risk, but I was perfectly content with that chance and the rest just came naturally. When you move through a transition and into a new chapter, then be open to receiving that change in the right spirit!

NOBLE SERVICE

Focusing on service is a great way to raise your vibration and get the positive energy flowing in your life. It adjusts your focus into helping others instead of being hyper focused on you and how you're feeling at any given moment. When you're focused on yourself, then you're fixated on pleasing your ego. When you're experiencing worry, stress, or anxiety, then adjust your attention in the direction of how you can help someone else in need. It not only alleviates any negative emotions experienced, but it uplifts you to be able to help someone else. This raises your vibration, which then attracts more positive circumstances to you. Suddenly the worries you had evaporate into the universe.

Having a connection with Heaven enables you to be able to help others in a positive way. When you're feeling out of sorts or unfocused, then reach out to others to see how you can assist them. This will help re-raise your vibration to a place of joy and contentment. You'll be on cloud nine when you are able to be of service and help someone out who truly needs it. At the same time be alert to not be taken advantage of by others due to your kindness. You've got to be sensitively sharp and on the ball to see through the dangers of someone taking advantage of you.

This is a narcissistic world with a grandiose sense of entitlement. This is a negative side effect to the rise of technology and social media giving everyone a voice. There is a fine line one walks between believing you deserve something, to carrying an arrogant air of privilege. If you do not merge into that middle ground mindset, then you'll get walked all over by everyone else.

Society, technology, your peers, the media and the Internet have trained human kind to display a self-absorbed aura. There are good selfless souls threaded around the world to counteract this attitude by being of service. This is not only to help others, but also to show that in the end good deeds prevail. No one warms up to a self-entitled brat, but instead they grow more distant to human kind. Direct your efforts into showing compassion and helping those in need or those who could use a friend and listening ear. This carries over to all aspects of your life.

WORKING FOR YOU

One awesome trait to successful self-employment requires that you be self-disciplined. You take your job seriously as if it were any other job. Instead of answering to someone else, you must answer to yourself. This is a good and bad thing depending on the dynamic. Who doesn't want to turn their hobby into a lucrative enterprise? One of the steps in doing that is to keep your side day job while you work at your hobby. If it truly is your hobby, then it won't feel like a drag to dive into it during off hours. This is another reason Heaven insists on everyone taking care of themselves on all levels. This way you don't experience early burn out. You have more energy and stamina to do both the regular income-making job, while you work at growing your side hobby business.

Don't quit your day job until you know for sure that you are consistently making enough to survive with the incoming money from your hobby. Ask your Spirit team to work with you full time in building your side business into full time work. The Archangels to call on for Heavenly assistance with this are Archangel Gabriel *(motivation manager)*, Archangel Nathaniel *(life purpose work)*, Archangel Michael *(eradicate fear)*, and Archangel Ariel *(abundance and supplies)*.

Know that it may take awhile before you are able to quit your regular day job. It could even take years, but if you believe it in enough and enjoy what you do, then eventually results will be forthcoming. It also won't feel like work doing what you love on the side. Building a business is like climbing a mountain until you reach the top. It will be a struggle at times, but it is a challenge that you can overcome with an endless reservoir of persistence, dedication, faith, confidence, and passion. This same mindset is the way you rule your life. In a sense, all souls are self-employed at heart. You manage you, your life, relationships, and your entire surroundings with the same commitment and enthusiasm you would as if it we're your own business. You are the chief executive of your life.

*C*hapter Six

Connect, Visualize, Create

*T*he power of visualization has been known to create extraordinarily magical results in your life. What assists in contributing to making great things happen are three central steps: *Optimistic Visualization, Paying Attention,* and *Taking Action.*

Optimistic Visualization – Using your imagination visually paint the picture of what you desire. Experience feelings associated with confidence and enthusiasm surrounding this visual, as if it is real and here in your life happening now. Avoid allowing doubts or worry to enter your mind as that can negate the process. When you experience negative feelings, then this energy multiplies causing more of that pessimism to come into your vicinity.

Optimistic visualization is about believing that what you want is coming to you with great veracity. Some achieve this by creating a vision board. A vision board or visual scrapbook is cutting out photographs of ideas of what you would like to have in your life. Pick up magazines to find these images or print them off your computer. You can use the vision board for whatever you choose from the kind of house you would like to live in, to the type of love interest you envision having, or for any other desires.

The reason some put a vision board together is because it helps them focus on what they want without forgetting about it or veering away from it. If they wake up every morning and the first thing they see is the vision board they made, then those images continue to build and seep into that person's consciousness. This is the same as those who have empowering words carved out and hanging around their house. It serves as a reminder so that they don't forget. The world is a busy place and people are distracted and rushing around. You're focused on negative feelings or on mundane practical tasks that need to get done. Soon you find that you've grown stuck in that routine energy. If you have these images and words up around your home, on your computer screen, or in a specific place where you see it regularly, then this triggers the essence, energy, and vision of what you want.

You've had another trying day at work arriving home beat and defeated. The first thing you see when you walk into your place is this board you created reminding you of the things you desire. It uplifts you a bit to see these images. Not everyone will want to have this vision board up on the mantle in their living room where all who come to visit see it. Perhaps it doesn't go with your décor. Find a place where you remember to catch a glimpse of it or have access to it. You can certainly shove it in your closet out of view from visitors, but don't forget it's there. Maybe stick it in a corner in your room or any other place that you know you'll remember having it.

The power of optimistic visualization is immensely helpful in obtaining your desires. Sometimes one can forget what's important when they are bogged down in the practicalities of their everyday life. They forget to daydream and visualize what will make them happy.

Daydreaming includes the dreams you have while sound asleep to the kinds of imaginative visuals you conjure up in your mind during waking hours. If you're someone who has frequent vivid dreams, then one of your dominant psychic senses is Clairvoyance.

Keep a notepad or journal near you to jot down key visuals that are in your dreams. Dreams tend to fade immediately or within minutes to an hour after waking. This is the benefit of writing it down quickly before you forget. Otherwise you'll find you're one of those people who later in the day says, "I had the greatest dream last night, but I can't remember any of it." You only remember the feeling it gave you. Your subconscious mind is where the greatest psychic input resides because your ego is asleep at that time. It's not getting in your way of receiving heavenly guidance and messages to discredit it.

Souls with an active imagination prone to daydreaming are that much closer to understanding the process of manifestation. A jaded blocked adult might tell a child, "Get your head out of the clouds and quit daydreaming."

This is tragic since the child has a better shot at manifesting their desires over the cynical adult.

Daydreaming requires one to be still and allow their thoughts to drift away from what is their current reality. Some daydream in order to escape an unhappy life. It's used as a safety device as they imagine what they wish their life would be like. Daydreaming is an escape in this scenario and used for their protection. If your home life is horrible or abusive, then it's not uncommon for that person to become a daydreamer of a life that is more pleasing to that person. It's also a great way to connect with Heaven and your Spirit team, since your thoughts are relaxed and moving towards what you desire. You're open to receiving psychic hits, messages, and guidance. Daydreaming is typically filled with positive wish-filled thoughts, which raise ones vibration and assists in manifesting good things in that individual's life. Great ideas come to you when you are in a daydream state since your connection to your Guides and Angels is stronger. You're not pushing for information while in a daydream state, so it flows through you naturally.

A vision board can be beneficial because it's there as a reminder to visualize what you want. The images you put on this board are right in front of you. Sometimes pulling the board down and gazing at the images at the end of the night or at the start of your day can help uplift you and put a smile on your face reminding you of what you desire. This uplifting feeling raises your vibration back up and what a great way to start each day.

Paying Attention - Pay attention to the guidance and messages that your Spirit team is relaying to you. If you're unclear on what your next step should be, then carve out some time where you can sit quietly in meditation.

Meditation helps you pick up on the guidance from spirit coming in. Some have expressed uncertainty on how to meditate or what it is. You move into a slight meditative state as you drift off to sleep at night without realizing it. It dissolves or reduces your waking ego and brings forth your consciousness. The answers come in clearer when you are calm, peaceful, centered, and in a setting that matches those traits. This is one of the many reasons that the angels advise that human souls be outdoors in nature. Nature settings are calming and it relaxes the mind. When the mind is relaxed, then the messages and guidance are picked up on in a clearer way. There is no distraction of the physical material world when you are hanging out in a low crowded nature setting. It takes some measure of discipline, since you need to shut off all noisy distractions such as television, cell phones, and boisterous people.

I've had cases where I sit down and Heaven's messages rush in out of nowhere, but then my phone buzzes near me and I have this urge to reach for it. After a number of times of being easily distracted I finally mumble, "Okay, that's it." I turn the phone off or put it in another room where I'm unable to hear it vibrating. My mind moves incredibly fast where I'm seeing and picking up on every nuance. I have to be disciplined about my surroundings when it's time for me to get down to business.

If you have trouble meditating due to not being focused, then create an atmosphere that works for you. This would be one that is set up in a way that moves you easily into a peaceful state. One way to do this is to find a place where there are no obtrusive distractions. Play some soft background music, light a candle, then sit and focus on it. Allow any mindless chatter or distracting energies to evaporate. Sitting or laying down works, but you might find that when you lay down that you drift off to sleep. It is okay if this happens since your Spirit team embeds messages into your consciousness. If clairvoyance is one of your stronger *Clairs*, then you might get the messages and guidance while dreaming.

If you're new to meditation, then don't worry if you're not receiving anything right away. The first number of times practice meditating without any intention of picking up on your Spirit team's guidance. When you strain to receive messages, then this blocks you from obtaining anything. Sometimes the guidance can come in after you've relaxed in meditation. You might have spent about fifteen minutes in this meditation state where you've cleared your mind and then you get up to continue on with your life. It's not uncommon for there to be a delay before you pick up on the messages. As you're getting ready for bed later on, suddenly the crystal clear Heavenly guidance comes rushing in through one of your Clair channels. You cry out, "That's it! That's the answer." You're swiftly filled with excitement and optimism, which is another sign that you've received Heavenly guidance, since there are no doubts, worry, or any other negative feeling involved when it's guidance from Heaven.

Taking Action – Take action and follow the guidance that your Spirit team has relayed to you. Sitting on your couch all day waiting for the blessing to ring your doorbell is highly unlikely to happen. You meet your Spirit team half way by asking them what steps you need to take next. Perhaps the message you receive is to re-send out your resume to a place you already sent it to, but received no response originally. Now your team is asking you to forget about all that and send it again. You send out your resume to the same place as your team requested, only this time you get a response asking you to come in for an interview or meeting.

Sometimes the messages and guidance might seem insignificant or trivial. I've relayed messages and guidance from my team asking me to discuss these basic steps of meditation and hammer home the nature setting again. That seems trivial initially, but as I illustrated it's for good reason that can help benefit your life. Rushing around stressed out wondering when your life will change is not going to allow you to pick up on Heaven's messages, which are delivered to assist in enhancing your life.

It is a tough process achieving what you've always wanted to do, but you can do it! Take it one step at a time and eventually you will master it. When it's something you really want to do, then there's nothing you cannot accomplish. It's that passion, drive, and persistence that is your winning card. It doesn't feel like a chore when it's something you love. You want to learn about the processes and different avenues you can take to reach that goal.

Chapter Seven

You Are Creative!

*W*hen you cannot seem to shake the uncomfortable rut of negative feelings plaguing and dominating your life, then dive into a creative project or hobby. Creative pursuits raise your vibration and lift the passion quotient within you. When you immerse yourself in a creative hobby, then this opens up your heart, enhances your soul, and brings joy into your life. Since immersing oneself raises your vibration, this attracts in good stuff and optimistic feelings to you outside of the creative hobby. If you do not have any creative interests, then it is time to look into obtaining one. Creative interests can be anything from picking up a paint-by-number set, to training yourself to play a musical instrument, to pottery making. There are endless ways to awaken the creative part of you.

Diving into creativity is a great way to shake yourself out of any funk you experience. It helps you navigate through the treacherous waters of human life. It assists you in finding innovative ways to solutions, which can carry over to other aspects of your life from the business arena to love relationships. It helps you to think outside of the box and showcase your originality because everything you're doing while being creative is solely you. It pulls out the deepest parts of your soul. A photographer is being creative by taking pictures. They might spend hours taking a variety of photos of different flowers in a garden. By doing this they see the beauty around them. These creative gifts come out of you and mirror what you have within. Your true nature is revealed back to you as a result.

You are wonderful and loved by God and the universe beyond measure and comprehension. How awesome is that to be loved no matter how you're feeling? All human souls desire to be loved and will seek it out in friendships, family members, colleagues and lovers. This is with the hope that these other souls will give you that all encompassing love. The love exists within you to begin with and can be conjured up naturally. This is God's love for you.

Creativity is a great reminder of who your soul truly is. It brings this love out of you. Creativity cures any boredom or lulls in your day while helping you to express yourself in positive ways. When human souls are bored, they tend to reach for an addiction. They might log online, surf the Internet pointlessly, visit a social media site, or log on to a phone app for human contact and stimulation that ceases to exist in their physical reality. You feel even more lonely and bored after hours of being unproductive. This becomes a bigger problem when you discover that this is how you spend every second of your day. If you didn't have that one step to check your page throughout the day, then you fear you might lose out on life. I've certainly had friends tell me, "Okay I've been on [social media] too much lately. I need to take a step back." They're going crazy inside realizing it's not fulfilling anything positive for them. This is more about someone who spends each day for months surfing the net out of lethargy while accomplishing nothing.

Artistic creative souls have a high attraction to abusing addictions and toxic substances. The same goes for those who are sensitive or psychically connected. If you are a sensitive, psychically connected, artistic, and creative, then the odds of you succumbing to a toxic vice or addiction runs higher than if you are one or the other. In many cases, having all of these traits go hand in hand with the super connected.

If you're a creative soul who regularly dives into artistic pursuits, then it's likely you have deeper psychic gifts than the average person. You may be aware of it or you are about to begin realizing the connection between both. When the artist doesn't create for long periods of time, then it can feel like you're running out of air. Creative inspiration is heavenly guided and influenced by Spirit. Your Spirit team plays a hand in it as well as the Archangel Gabriel, who joins the creative being to assist in the inspiration and motivation process. Archangel Gabriel is the hierarchy angel who oversees all creative souls who choose to turn their gifts into a lifelong hobby or career.

Artists are sensitive and can access and channel this inspiration often without knowing it. Channeling comes naturally to them, regardless if they are a believer in something outside of themselves or not.

If you fit this description, know that you are immensely gifted, rather than cursed. The curse is when you feel unable to control the access of information or creativity that pours into you. Therefore, you find that you reach for substances that might be considered an addiction. This is merely a way of pointing out what one needs to be aware of.

Part of your soul's growth is to gain control of your ego. This may take a lifetime depending on one's individual journey. You can become a master at being disciplined and yet you still find yourself tumbling down the rabbit hole every once in awhile. When that happens, call on Heaven for support. Don't beat yourself up over it. I have been a lifelong addict, but others claim or protest to view me as being completely together, strong, and independent. It doesn't matter, because the addiction gene runs right through the human development part of my soul. It's something I wrestle with no matter how connected I am. I do my best to stay focused and do what I need to do. Over time, I learned to talk myself out of reaching for an addiction until the cravings grew to be less. Luckily, my hard addictions were in my early twenties. I got it all out of my system so to speak, yet the addictive behavior is still there just below the surface. I have mastered the art of keeping it tempered and quiet through daily work, discipline, and effort.

Many well-known artists, musicians, and actors are unable to control the input of information, which tampers with their psyche. This drives them to drug, alcohol, or any other addiction to numb it all. One of the ways to avoid falling into an ocean of addiction is to find avenues to channel your creativity and gifts in a positive way. Take up a side hobby to unleash your positive gifts through an artistic endeavor. I worked with a well-known actress for many years who paints when she's not acting in front of the camera. Painting is another form of creative expression.

Actors feel more in control when they are working and inhabiting a character on stage or film. This keeps them out of trouble to an extent. If they're not working, which many are not on a regular basis, they find other positive avenues of creative expression. When you are working on a creative project, you are less likely to resort to addictive substances. Creative expression brings you joy and an internal rushed high feeling that raises your vibration. This rush that you experience is your natural connection line with Heaven.

You may feel like an oddball or weird, but avoid placing too much emphasis on labeling yourself. Others may ridicule or criticize you for being different. They might call you inappropriate names, but pay no mind. It is better to be different than to be a clone that follows the herd. You are special and thank God for that. You have a high receptivity to your environment, so you will want ensure that your surroundings are controlled and that you incorporate some measure of discipline. If you have too much rigid control, then this can inhibit your artistic creative side. Finding a happy balance with everything in life is what contributes to a positive energy flow. Be expressively creative while running your life like a strict executive.

The negatives that happen to this are that creative types are also all about experiencing and experimenting to one degree or another. It's best to work on keeping your research on a level that does not bring on an addiction. I am a writer, author, storyteller and entertainer. Couple this with me being a former addict with an ongoing addictive personality, so research has been my middle name. I would not just do something new a little bit. I would do it a lot becoming an obsessive-compulsive mess.

Artistic pursuits and creative expression is a great way to reduce or eliminate blocks in your life. It's a positive healthy way to channel and direct negative, stifled, and stuck energy. By diving into creative pursuits, you're releasing the negative energy and these blocks in the process. You're also awakening your inner child, which resides in a higher state than your ego. Consider finding a creative hobby or interest that brings you joy. Creativity enhances your life force and lifts your confidence level. You may even find that your creative project soon turns into life purpose work where it brings in supplemental income, or becomes a full time self employed career. Some creative pursuits can include hobbies such as photography, painting, writing, playing music, singing, dancing, puzzles, or any measure of arts and crafts.

Writing is a great way to be creative and express your inner self. You don't have to necessarily write a published book. It can be something that you write for the sake of release. Writing is fantastic therapy! You can write your own manuscript or keep a regular journal. Join writing groups you feel comfortable in enough to share your work with others, or to have a meeting with like minded individuals that share your interests. If you're shy for in-person meetings or you don't have the time to travel to group settings, then look for online forums and groups where you can communicate via the Internet. This is one of the plusses to having access to technology.

Keep a personal diary when you're going through transitions or just want to jot down day-to-day stuff. You can email it to yourself. For example, use the subject line: Diary+Date *(Diary 12-25-15)*. Jot down anything that comes to you about that day, what you're going through, how you're feeling or anything at all, then email it to yourself. Create a folder in your email box marked "Journal" or "Diary" and file each one in there. Choose to do what you want with it at a later date or just keep it for your eyes only. If you can speak, then you can write.

Every soul has some measure or range of creative gifts within them, even if you never honed in on that aspect of yourself. It might come out in ways that you never expected or in a manner that you wouldn't think to equate as one being creative. It comes out in a variety of ways such as being birthed out of the mundane and the practical. It can be the way you organize your house, to working on a puzzle, to taking that extra step to ensure that your emails are centered, justified, or in the right font. Creativity can be in the way you speak to others, whether that is on the phone, at your job, or on a stage to an audience.

Although the news media is responsible for a major influence on the darkness of one's ego in humanity, the media in general is a great outlet for a creative sensitive to pursue work in. Many have agreed to an Earthly life at this time in order to transmit their work in a much easier way than it would have been pre-Internet days. During pre-Internet days other people had a hold on preventing any creative artist from getting their work out to the public. Now most anyone can get their work out there with strong effort, diligence, and hard work. Depending on what your creative work entails, you may still need a team around you to some extent such as an agent, publicist, manager, etc.

While in one sense you are the manager of your life and your work, but in another it is helpful to have supportive professional objective parties around you for feedback when unleashing your art to the world. A friend is great to bounce stuff off of as long as the friend is someone you can trust. They are someone you can take constructive criticism from without getting upset or allowing it to damage your connection. The flip side is this friend should not be the type who is negative or jealous of you either. You likely being a sensitive should be able to pick up on any hint of dishonesty or malice from anyone when it comes to your art. It should be a given that you surround yourself with supportive friends, but sometimes even with the best supportive friendships they may develop resentment when they witness your success.

The one drawback to being able to put your creative work out into the world is marketing dollars. You can put your art into the world for sale, but if no one knows that it's out there and available, then it might feel as if your work was done for nothing. Unless you've got a huge trust fund or have made enough money at your day job to be able to do your creative life purpose work, then it can be challenging. True creative artists enjoy doing their work regardless of that. It's certainly helpful to have marketing dollars to promote your work, or to make enough money with it where you can quit your day job. The creative artist who lives and breathes their work will still do it because they enjoy it. It's fulfilling and rewarding to them even if in the back of their mind they would like to make enough money to be able to do it full time.

Even if you are not immediately financially rewarded, take the time to acknowledge and recognize the beautiful work you've accomplished, as that will be its own reward. Give to yourself in some positive way for every job well done. This assists in boosting your self-worth and vibration, which are both magnets for attracting in good stuff!

Be your most genuine and real self, but this goes without saying that your work should also be authentic. Authenticity is you being your most honest self without fear of judgment or criticisms. Avoid making changes or compromising because someone disagrees with any part of who you are and how you choose to express that. At the same time, understand the benefits of constructive feedback, but don't marinate in it to the point where you feel it's negotiating how you express your artistic truth. When you bargain this honesty, then the heart essence put into the work is lost. It doesn't feel right and nor does it feel like you. You want to step away from the drama surrounding that. This is in order to clear your mind when you find that you're moving into people pleasing to make others happy.

Find the right balance between accepting others feedback and keeping your work genuine. The point of getting a second pair of objective eyes on your work put out to the public is because when you're heavily mired in a project or anything for that matter, you don't see the possible hidden mistakes that could be present. There is a benefit to having compassionate, yet helpful input. Ask your team to guide you to the right people who can give honest feedback. There is a surplus of websites and companies devoted to offering services of every variety for a small fee. Sometimes this is the best route over giving it to a friend or acquaintance, since that becomes a conflict of interest. The one hired is objective and emotionally detached from what you're doing. This makes it a great test to see how a stranger reacts to it since your work is going out to strangers in the end as it is.

There will be times where it can be challenging to get motivated to do something you love. There are a variety of factors that could contribute to a lack of motivation. You're overworked, tired, stressed, depressed or have no support system. You have too much going on in your life around you. This is tampering chaotic and distractive energy enclosing in on your mind that it's difficult to find that space where motivation resides.

Some ways to get motivated are through relaxation. Take a time out to clear your space and remove any excess noise and distraction energy around you whether that is from people, your schedule, to any technological devices such as your phone or Internet. Turn off or temporarily remove phone apps that you hang out on to the point that you find that it occupies a great deal of your time. These are time wasters that block creative flow.

Sometimes doing busy work can help motivate you

to do what you really want to do, because it's getting your mind charged up. Creative people understand this concept, since they have wrestled with creative blocks at one time or another. A writer is ready to sit down and start writing, but experiences a block having no clue what to write about. What do they do? They clean the house, dust, vacuum, and organize. There are positive benefits to this, which includes implementing great Feng Shui. Feng Shui is an ancient Chinese art that contributes to the positive flow of good energy moving through all aspects of your life including your home and your soul. Some hire a professional Feng Shui artist to help them organize their home. This includes setting up your furniture in a manner that assists in attracting in good fortune. In the case where you're doing the busy work that consists of cleaning your house, this helps with the positive flow of energy, but isn't necessarily the art of Feng Shui. It's still an encouraging step in the right direction.

Writing or creating in a clean organized environment contributes to more precise focus, relaxation, motivation, and it helps in attracting in success. You want to make sure you don't find that you've wasted hours on this busy work. You've got so good at cleaning the house that the day is over and you have no energy left to create. To get motivated takes discipline and you have to manage your life and the decisions you make like a top business executive.

Feeling overwhelmed can prevent you from finding that spark of motivation. You're looking far out in the distance at the end result of what you want to do. This makes the goal seem daunting or intimidating so you talk yourself out of doing it and putting it off. Breaking your ultimate goal into baby steps is the way to go.

I call on the Archangel Uriel who lights the path that is unseen. Archangel Uriel will show me one step at a time when working on a book. I'll be asked to cover one topic, and then once that's accomplished he illuminates the next step. Before I know it, what I set out to achieve is complete.

Uriel offers awesome creative impressions by dropping these light bulb ideas into your mind. You have a creative idea, but then you grow overwhelmed as to how you're going to accomplish it. This is because you're seeing it far out in the distance, which will feel overpowering. Take it one small step at a time and try not to think of the end result. This is a delay tactic the ego will impose upon you by making you believe that it's not possible to do. A rock climber understands its goal is to reach the top, but they're merely focusing on one step climb upwards at a time. They're not thinking, "I've got to get up there to the top. That seems so far. I can't do it."

Others complain about what's going on in their life and how it is not up to their standards. I ask them if they've asked for help. They will say, "Oh you're right! Okay, I will do that."

Talk to your Spirit team regularly and ask for help as needed, including with creative ideas. When you notice there is no movement and you begin to feel discouraged, then ask Heaven to boost your faith and show you signs that movement is forthcoming.

Signs and symbols are put in your path by your Spirit team to let you know they are with you and do hear your requests. It can also be to give you clues as to what they are trying to communicate to you. When you're ferociously requesting help and wondering if you're being heard, they will do things such as drop feathers, objects of meaning, or coins around you to let you know they got your message. Since they cannot pick up the phone to call you or send you an email, they resort to manipulating the energy in order to let you know they hear you loud and clear, or to get a specific message across. You are not being ignored and that should bring you peace of mind.

THE PERSONAL ALTAR

Creating a personal alter is a wonderful way to rouse your creativity. Awakening the creative part of you is beneficial because it unleashes pent up closed off repression. When left unchecked this can be a breeding ground for illnesses, diseases, and other negative attributes. There are hundreds of ways to begin the process of setting the creative part of you free. Creating a personal alter is one way, as it can be used as a place of focus when you're in a scattered state. This alter can be used for whatever you choose. Many spiritual people like to create this space for prayer, meditations, or readings. You decide what you will use it for.

Find a space or a corner in your home somewhere to set up a small table, which you will use to place important sacred items on it that have meaning to you. You can place candles on it, crystals, divination tools, incense, sage, flowers, and/or little statues of deities that have some significance to you. My personal alter is a double level covered square table. Hidden underneath the table reside hundreds of card decks I use for readings whenever I choose to doubly confirm information I'm getting psychically. When you create your sacred space, you will want to cleanse and purify it on occasion. You can do this by sage smudging. Light a bit of sage and move it all around you, then the table and area. Say a mental prayer with the intention that you are clearing this space of any lower energy allowing only the light to enter. You can use this space for prayer, to connect, to meditate, to get focused, or for whatever you choose.

Because this is a sacred space, you will want to ensure that it is protected. This means not only clearing it through prayer or the occasional Sage smudging, but avoid placing other items on it. You're rushing around or you come home from work and immediately toss your car keys onto the sacred space table. Treating the space as a sacred one means you keep it protected and clear of other energies. When you toss your car keys on it, you're contaminating the sacred space with any negative energy that latched itself onto the keys. When you're driving the busy roads, then you're picking up on other energies such as abusive drivers or toxic people in other cars passing you. Ensure that you avoid putting anything else on the table that is not considered sacred to you.

THE JOY OF RECEIVING

Give yourself a break and practice the joy and love of receiving. Many spiritual or compassionate people have the qualities of being a selfless giver. While this is a magnificent heavenly trait to have, you can create an imbalance when that is all you are doing. In order to bring balance into your life, be open to receive in your life as well. When someone wants to do something nice for you for a change, then welcome that with open arms. Those who are predominately givers tend to wrestle with the joy of receiving. They might fall into the category of someone taking advantage of them. Never mistake kindness for weakness.

Receiving is also giving to yourself where you are the receiver. It's treating yourself to something you love such as a weekend getaway somewhere or a spa day if you enjoy being pampered. Whatever it is that makes you smile to receive, then go for it and give to yourself.

When you balance giving and receiving gestures, then this uplifts your mood, raises your vibration, and awakens your inner child who is bursting with creativity. If you are the kind of person who gives too much or receives without giving, then this creates an imbalance in your life. Work on balancing the giving part of your nature with receiving.

Sometimes you work hard feeling like you're being ignored, or that there are no blessings coming out of this hard work. What can be a possible block is this feeling you're experiencing. It's that deep inside you feel undeserving of blessings on some level. Know that you deserve blessings of abundance and good. Allow Heaven to bestow you with compensation for what you contribute to others and the world. When you open your arms to receive abundance, then it is easier to assist others when you're taken care of first.

In some ways, this is where you're spread too thin, but you drop everything to help a friend, loved one, or family member whenever they ask. If you're not taken care of or in a comfortable place, then you feel resentful for having to help. Receiving is just as important as giving. Therefore, ensure there is a healthy balance on both ends.

Chapter Eight

Fire Up Your Inner Child

*Y*ou grow older, your body ages, and you become more hip to the idea that you need to be responsible and disciplined if you want to survive living on the planet as pain free as possible. You have bills to pay, clothes to buy, and food to eat. How far in before you've lost yourself in physical Earthly demands?

You know you're beginning to lose yourself when your relationships with those around you grow distant or fall apart. It's when you're running on empty, stressed, tired, or both. The way human life is today is that you cannot sit on the couch all day drinking beer, app chatting, and texting even though many do that including myself. You need to get a job, make money, and support yourself. You'll want to keep a fine line between doing that and not losing yourself to the point where your inner child is trapped until its release when you pass on.

Your inner child is the person you were before age ten. It is the innocent all loving part of you as a child that had no judgment or criticisms of other people. Those criticisms came upon you through your environment and at the hands of those who heavily influenced you. If you grew up in a community where the people were racist, then the chances of you developing this racism trait are higher than anyone else. You were not born racist and nor were you prejudice against anyone and their life choices. This goes for any sort of bias from political affiliations, religion, or hatred of someone's sexual orientation. None of that exists with your inner child. Your inner child is the part of you that has the most access to God, because it is all love, joy, and peace. Your inner child is the one who knows how to have fun. It longs for this release and fun, if only your ego would pull that part of you back out to play again. When the dark ego dominates and grows lost in the physical world, your inner child screams for attention and love. Diving into creative artistic pursuits is a great way to fire up your inner child. When your inner child remains buried under rubble, then feelings of emptiness and loss begin to rise. Some go through these feelings of being lost during pinnacle times in their life. It can be brought upon due to a loss of any kind, such as the loss of a job, a friendship, a lover, or any other loss to something that gave you a sense of security or happiness.

Lost feelings for a prolonged period of time can also indicate that you're moving through a transition that will eventually lead to an awakening. This awakening is where you gain clarity on everything around you and what you need to do. There is no time limit when moving through a transition or a personal evolution. It can take one month, one year, or three years. Allow what is intended to evolve without interference. Go about life business and avoid pushing for anything to happen.

Your inner child is who you were before all of the layers of trauma and life experiences jaded you. It was when you saw life without judgment or critique. You saw life through the lens of innocence and fun. It was before human tampering made you despise anyone who is different from you. Those who despise someone that is different we're not that way when they were four years old. It was their caregivers, peers, community, and society influence that taught all of that stuff. If God raised you, then you would've grown up to see the love in all souls. You would exude love and joy full time.

When you were born, you were immensely psychic, and filled with overflowing feelings of love, joy, and peace. You were wide eyed ready to absorb everything around you. You saw the beauty in life, in the colors, and in the trees. You were also a sponge absorbing the environment you were growing up in.

If your parents were the type who would constantly argue with one another in front of you, then this hostile energy is absorbed and becomes a part of you. If you're caregivers and the society you live in were prejudice in any form, then this rubs off on you and you begin to believe this is the way it is. If someone is different from you, then you must be repulsed by them. Hate is not something you were born with, but your environment teaches it to you.

The souls who enter into this life from the various realms in Heaven are born into an Earthly life for a bigger purpose. They evolve at a rapid pace than a newborn soul would. They're the ones who might grow up in a toxic environment, but have higher awareness and psychic intuition to know that the way everyone else is behaving or thinking is wrong. They might be considered the black sheep of the family, or be considered an outcast, or weird. You are none of those things, but in fact are more important than you realize. You are and always will be a child of God with a greater purpose than perhaps someone who is having their first Earthly life run.

You may have a growing body or an adult body, but inside this physical case beneath all of the layers of your experiences resides your inner child. Your inner child is buried underneath an avalanche of experiences, lifestyle choices, and human development interference. When you had a negative, toxic, or abusive experience, then this is seared into your consciousness even if you continue on with life having great times. This child within you cries out for fun whenever you're feeling any negative emotion. Your inner child is psychic and operating from a higher vibration than any other part of you. This is why Heaven urges others to find that part of you and bring them back out. Your inner child is pure joy to be around, so let this part of you run free once in awhile in order to bring you back.

HUGGING AND TOUCH

Hugging and touching have immense healing properties to the soul. It awakens your inner child, which is also connected to the creative part of you. Are you overworked, stressed, depressed, or angry? Hug others more and allow them to hug you. Hugging lowers your blood pressure, relieves stress, releases the brain chemical Oxytocin. This contributes to positive bonding or otherwise known as the love hormone. Hugging reminds you that we're all on the same side. Many of the cure all remedies for so many issues reside within you. Hugs are one of the various activities that promote positive health. And hugs don't cost anything. They're free!

If you're willing to part with a hug, then do it more often. Hug your friend, your lover, and even your pet! Unless your pet is a gold fish, then you can just pucker up and blow kisses at it from the glass of the aquarium. Animals are souls and crave the hug of another. Hugging is one of the many great vibration enhancers. For a brief moment your soul can breathe while in the midst of a hug. It tears away any off-putting ions that latch itself onto the aura around your spirit. You experience release and you understand what freedom feels like.

Everyone needs a hug whether they like to admit it or not. The most toughened human soul needs that love to tear down the walls they've built around their heart. You've likely come across someone who you try to hug and they clam up or turn into a brick wall barely giving back the hug. They're terribly uncomfortable being touched as it's not something they likely grew up getting enough of. They hardened over time at some point in their life.

Many are angry, depressed, or feeling any other kind of emotion that disconnects your soul from a feeling of joy, peace, or love. Those qualities are traits which are innate inside of you, but buried so far deep it can't climb out of the hole it's trapped itself in. The world needs a war on hugs. If you're going to complain about something, then complain that you're receiving too much love, hugs, and kisses from the world. There are millions of nerve endings in the human skin and to experience touch activates these nerves prompting you to raise your vibration.

BRING ON THE JOY

Joy is one of the highest vibrating energies that exist next to love. When someone laughs into hysterics, you sense the infectious energy. Suddenly strangers around that person light up with a smile. Someone else's energy will affect others around them. If they're being negative, then that will transfer. If they're infectiously giggly, then that will transfer. Seeing the fun and lightheartedness in situations raises your vibration. It lightens the heavy loaded burdens of stress. When your vibration is high, you attract in brighter circumstances to you. If you're stuck in negative feelings, then call upon your Spirit team and ask them to help in elevating your soul into a happier space. Request that they guide you to getting back into the joy of your life again. Radiating with joy is what brings more of that good stuff to you. No one wants to be around a miserable stressed out and depressed grump. Feeling joy while visualizing your desires is what helps the manifestation process take place more quickly too. Archangel Jophiel is the hierarchy angel to call on to bring more joy and beauty into your life.

The working class is breaking their back to put

food on the table and take care of their families and loved ones. They're being run ragged into the ground. This is thanks to human decision to work people like dogs. I've had so many conversations with the working class over the years and I've heard their common understandable complaints. I wonder how many politicians have truly heard the stories I have or even care. If they have, then they would've implemented change by now.

I'm an advocate for hard work as is Heaven, but this means working hard while incorporating regular time outs to decompress and spend with your loved ones. This isn't about working one day a month while doing nothing the rest of the time. This is working smarter schedules. Although the five day forty hour work week is excessive, it was much worse pre-1900's when people were expected to work 10-16 hours a day. Soon it was realized that it needed to be cut shorter such as creating the "Weekend" off to give people a break. Now even that's not enough since lives are busier than ever. People are getting smarter and hip to the fact that the soul and body need more adequate time for rest and relaxation. It's currently not enough, because by the time the weekend comes around people spend the first day getting all of that practical stuff they did not have time to get done during the week. The second and last day is spent burned out and lounging around. Finally on the third day, they're energetic and ready to do something fun, but alas it's time to head back into the office.

At least several times a month incorporate playtime and personal time. This is essential to your overall health and wellbeing. This will also increase productivity and decrease worldwide health issues, not to mention help the crumbling of all types of relationship connections. This personal time isn't used to go grocery shopping, gassing up the car, or gym time, which is a necessity and wasted on one of the weekend days off. It's to be used to connect with loved ones, relax, rejuvenate, take a day trip, or any other fun activity that helps you let go and release.

Heaven watches millions of people rushing to and from a job burned out and running on little sleep. It saddens them to have this aerial view of so many detached souls who are unhappy deep down. It's no wonder there is a rise in disconnection from God. Heaven demands that all souls take a time out to enjoy regular bouts of personal luxury time. When you include fun and relaxation in your life, then when you head back to work, you're more energetic and focused. Your soul is crying in pain when it runs on any permanent negative emotion. Luxuries are a necessity. Stress, anxiety, and depression are examples of symptoms that crush your soul. This energy shoots into your physical body causing an array of issues. It also merges into your aura and touches other people's auras around you that absorb that.

ENERGY DRAINING

Have a zero tolerance policy for any meanness, negativity, or drama from anyone. There is a difference between loving someone from afar without getting caught up in their drama or toxic energy, to choosing to keep them at arm's length if you don't want them to go away. It might be a family member, parent, sibling, friend, or colleague. It can be someone where it's seemingly not easy to cut the person out of your life permanently. You love the goodness in them, but no one should put themselves in a position where they are a punching bag.

Someone might not be mean towards you directly, but they harshly complain about other people to you where you end up feeling down or worn out after communicating with them. Having your energy drained by others is real. This is why those on the receiving end grow weakened, annoyed, or rubbed the wrong way. Those who are doing the energy draining are not necessarily aware they are, because this type of energy makes one clouded.

You can be an exceptionally good compassionate person yourself and not realize when you're in the midst of behaving in a negative way. You're having a physical human experience and it's going to happen once in awhile. You want to be aware of that when it happens. This is about someone who is always negative or toxic every time you connect with them.

When negative energy from someone else is around you, then you want to steer clear of it and not become consumed by it. If you drown in it, then this will bring you down, darken your aura, and lower your vibration. All of these phrases mean the same thing. If you are a sensitive or in tune to energies beyond the physical world, then you cannot deny how it makes you feel when you're around someone who is toxic. You can have love for them and still choose to not engage with them full time. Connect with them in small doses and then wrap it up and excuse yourself that you need to leave. They might react in a tantrum, but don't fall into guilt. You have to think of you first.

Everyone is living their own path and no one can live it for them. If someone chooses to head down a self-destructive path, no one can stop them. They have to want to change on their own. You can be polite when they reach out to you, but blow in and out of there quickly. This way they're not around long enough to infiltrate your area with their toxins.

The key is to say, "I have love for them and wish them well, but we don't engage much. When we do, I stand in a place of emotional detachment."

Energy draining is a major issue in the lives of millions of people around the world. It pushes them to pop pills to sleep, or pop them to wake up to continue on. It lures them into toxic addictions such as alcohol, food, and even drugs. You can wake up feeling alive and joyful, then you get in your car to head to work and the traffic is so bad that by the time you arrive at work you feel drained and dejected. The planet is overflowing with people and so many of them understand the fight to keep on going every day morning and night. Others underestimate how bad traffic can be when they find a job and a place to live. You might think you live fifteen minutes away from work, but that is until you neglect to take into account that the commute can be thirty to forty minutes, and that's on a good day. This is a major energy drainer and so are some of the choices one makes in their life. This can be from who you associate with from friendships to love relationships. Working with one bad apple can spoil your work life.

When you notice these circumstances happening, then you want to begin the process of considering the options you can make to alleviate this kind of stress. You do not want to spend years in a situation that drains your energy since this is equal to draining your life force. Not to mention the long-term health issues that can arise and the blocks erected between yourself and Heaven's guidance.

*C*hapter Nine

Assertiveness, Aggression, Passive Aggression

*W*hen one is angry or upset, the human ego will display three different traits: Aggression, passive-aggression, or assertiveness.

The highest and most effective energy form of getting your point across when you're upset or need to correct a wrong is by displaying assertiveness.

Aggression is being directly hostile when you confront someone. You're a militant bully with the mantra that it is your way or the high way and no other opinion is allowed. Aggression primarily comes from fear or ego. It is fear that you are not being heard or the person you're directing that aggression towards is not going to listen to you. It can also come from high anxiety brought on in artificial ways such as consuming too much caffeine where you're bouncing all over the place in agitated aggression.

Aggressive force is your ego wanting to make sure that the person you're directing this force towards understands that you are in charge. You will convey that point by any means necessary. It's attempting to dominate someone with severe force to get that person to go along with your point.

Someone who screams their argument at someone while pointing their finger repeatedly at you is someone who is being aggressive. When you're aggressive you have a sense of entitlement with some self-righteousness mixed in for fun.

A man sees someone moving in on his love partner, and the man becomes a bully and starts to physically shove the person who is making the move on his mate. This is aggressive behavior and it is also someone with high testosterone. It's innate in the male species, so there is nothing to be ashamed of. It's being brought up here as a guide to keep it under control as much as possible. I definitely understand since it's been known that I can be pretty aggressive at times. The content my Spirit team relays are for me too! It is instinctual in the male species to react aggressively to ensure others understand you've marked your territory.

Passive aggression is just as bad as aggression, except that passive aggression is indirect. You're upset with a love partner, but you don't say anything or tell them that you are angry or bothered by something they did. Instead you keep it bottled up until it explodes in underhanded ways. The passive aggressive person will pout and mope whenever you're around. You'll sense something is wrong, but when you ask them if everything is okay, they appear cold and distant holding in their emotion, "I'm fine." They throw up a wall that makes them inaccessible and thus becoming submissive. This person may have lower testosterone and more estrogen, but they could also be more sensitive or afraid of confrontation erupting. Your thoughts and feelings do matter. It's important to express them when possible by being assertive.

The male species typically has a good deal of testosterone and therefore comes off aggressive when upset, while the female species has more estrogen and therefore can come off passive aggressive when upset. Either gender has displayed both aggression and passive aggression regardless of how much testosterone or estrogen one has. The reasoning for laying out the examples in this way is a generality. This way of reacting to something one is upset about is part of the human make-up, but it is one that can be reined in. Men see a drop in their testosterone levels as they age, while women see a drop in their estrogen levels and rise in testosterone.

I was jogging through a quiet residential area at night and suddenly a dog came at me. I stopped thrown off guard and hopped back a couple steps. A woman yanked the dog back with the leash at the same time. The woman said with warmth and kindness, "Don't you mind him. He just likes you cause you've got a lot of testosterone."

She was right since when active men continuously work out and exercise it starts to raise their testosterone levels. This can also contribute to the aggressiveness that comes out at times.

The passive aggressive person doesn't necessarily communicate with you with words. When they do finally talk with you, they make comments that start to sound as if they are indirectly attacking you or giving you back handed compliments. It takes you awhile, maybe even weeks before you realize, "Wait a minute, you're mad at me. What's wrong?"

The partner exuding passive aggressive behavior is unable to articulate what's wrong, so they become aloof, cold, and distant with you. They might be sad and slouch whenever you're around. If you're a sensitive or someone in tune, then you can pick up on this energy like nobody's business. Someone who is not in tune has no clue the other person's mad, so it can take much longer to realize it.

Passive aggression also comes from fear, where the person is afraid to voice what's wrong, as they don't want to rock the boat or start a fight. They're not fans of confrontation and it's easier to just not say anything and mope around the issue. The problem is that keeping this anger or upset inside for prolonged periods of time can fester and cause potential health issues. It's better to get it out even if someone doesn't want to hear it. You can articulate what's wrong with compassion and assertiveness.

If you're afraid to say something, then write it out. You don't have to email it to the person you're upset with. Email it to a trusted friend or to yourself. It's important to get those feelings out of you. Whenever one of my close loved ones and trusted ones we're going through a heartbreaking relationship split with someone who left them, they would have the urge to call the leaver or send them an email full of angry and upset tirades. They would send it to me saying, "Should I send this to them?" I'd of course say, "Oh no, don't say that. Write out everything to your heart's content, but just send it to yourself or me so you feel like you're getting it out of you."

Sometimes they would send it to me and then send it to their partner that left them as well. It always backfires in their face where they come back to me. "I should've listened to you. Now it's worse than ever!"

When someone has chosen to leave you, there is nothing you can do or say to change that person's mind. They've already decided and it's in motion. They've more than likely decided long before they took that step to let you in on it. It's best to give them what they want and that is to be separated from you. If it's meant to be, they will come back and then you can decide whether to go for another round or move on.

One thing to consider is that you should feel safe enough to talk openly with your love mate. A relationship is supposed to be you and this person against the world. If you can't talk about things openly with one another, then who can you talk to about that stuff?

Getting an aggressive person to calm down is challenging since the aggressive person is heated. When you are dealing with an aggressive person, you're dealing with someone who is disconnected from their centered higher self. They are in no position to reason with, so it's best to get out of their line of fire and wait until they cool off.

The passive aggressive person is challenging to deal with also, because the wall they put up is impossible to pull down in order to get them to open up. The person they're being that way with starts to feel rejected by them. This creates an even bigger distance between both people.

The souls who have incarnated from the heavenly realm of the wise ones on the other side or who are part of the Indigo Generation tend to have high amounts of aggressive behavior, but so do newborn baby souls who are having their first Earthly life run. They are unable to grasp proper etiquette and communication. As a Wise One, I have been guilty of displaying aggression since Wise One's have a bit of a temper at times. Their goal is to work on moving that aggression into assertiveness. As I've grown older, I've found that I've been more successful at being assertive over aggressive, even though it will freely come out here and there as its part of the Wise One/Indigo nature. I've certainly also had moments of passive aggression, but that's mostly in past love relationships. I am a sensitive and did not want to rock the boat with the person I'm involved with. This stems from an abusive childhood where I was trained to go along with someone just to please the abusive person. It's taken a lifetime of working on dissolving that or at least greatly reducing that behavior.

In the end, most everyone displays aggression, passive aggression, and assertiveness at one time or another. Be aware when you are displaying aggressive or passive-aggressive behavior, and then begin the process of shifting that energy into assertiveness.

An aggressive person can use blunt force or derogatory name calling to get someone to hear their point. They might say something like, "You're an *(expletive)*! Anyone with half a brain knows that doesn't work!" Whereas someone who displays assertive behavior will speak the truth directly with strength, but it is intertwined with compassion and understanding where one is open to compromise. You're not talking at someone to force your belief down someone's throat. Instead, the assertive person is talking with the other person as if they're on the same level.

An assertive person will say something like, "I understand your point, but it would be more effective if we did it this way, because then you're not excluding anybody."

A passive aggressive person wouldn't say anything even though they're bothered by something. They would willingly go along with what they disagree with, even though deep down they're unhappy about it. No one would know they're unhappy about it, because the passive aggressive person isn't telling them they have a problem.

Assertiveness is the goal to thrive for when angry or upset about something. When you display assertiveness, you accomplish what you want. An assertive person is firm, stands their ground, but they work with and include the other person they're attempting to come to a resolution with. The assertive person is calm, strong, and composed, but not unresponsive, which would be passive aggressive. They are also not a tough bully, which is aggression. The assertive person is a relaxed centered person who is also direct in their communication with what they want to accomplish. They speak clearly and concisely without being heated and slamming things around.

When there is conflict, the best way to handle it is by being assertive. Call upon your Spirit team to give you confidence if you're feeling passive aggressive. If you're feeling constantly aggressive, then ask your team to help you in relaxing. Request they assist you in stating your point without hurting, upsetting, or walking over anyone.

During my Film Production days in the Entertainment Business, I was working with a Production Supervisor on a Sony Pictures movie. At times of high stress, she would come off abusive with her staff. Ironically, she wasn't like that with me, but that's usually the case as I have low tolerance for abuse. I naturally have the stance of someone demanding respect that most people give that when I enter a room. I became close with her since I tend to get along well with the extroverted tempestuous difficult types that rub others the wrong way. Perhaps it's because I'm a little tempestuous and difficult? When I noticed she first stepped out of line with a crew member, I pulled her to the side with calm assertiveness and said, "That was harsh."

She pulled back struck by the statement. Mist glazed over her eyes as she revealed vulnerability. "Was I?" She continued, "I totally respect you. This is why I need you to tell me and smack me into shape if you see me doing that."

Afterwards, when I noticed her slipping into rude, hostile, antagonistic, bullying aggression with a crew member, I'd walk by and give her a little wink with a wagging of the finger. Soon she began to be cognizant of when she might be crossing the line on her own. It was a proud moment seeing that she wanted to change and become better at dealing with others professionally with assertiveness, rather than aggression. It wasn't her intention to be nasty as deep down she is a good giving person, but needed to be taught tools and other effective ways of communicating that wouldn't alienate or turn others off. Unfortunately, spiritual concepts such as this one are not something that is taught in school.

There was one minor incident I recall that happened with a Production Assistant where this woman slammed at him about it just as I happened to be walking into the room. Minutes later, when she was alone with me she asked me if she was too harsh there. I explained that she was and that she can get her point across with greater success by being assertive. "People will respect you more and it'll boost morale."

After those instances, I began to notice her softening over the course of the film shoot. She grew to become friendlier, fun, giving, and all smiles with the crew. She was still as much in control and strong as before, but she didn't need to convey that strength through abuse. Before that, she was notoriously known as a mean taskmaster that was whipping the crew into shape as if they were slaves. I was proud of watching her shift from aggression to assertiveness in the way that she supervised the crew by the end of the shoot.

If human souls kept their ego in check, there would be peace on Earth. No wars, fighting, hate, or causing others pain. It would be as if you were back in Heaven where those negative factors don't exist. Keeping your ego in check is by displaying assertiveness, instead of aggression and passive aggression.

Chapter Ten

Improve Your State of Mind

Every soul has varying degrees of psychic abilities regardless if that soul believes in it or not. You are born with heightened Clair channels, but somewhere along your human life development, these Clair channels become clogged due to negative influences. The purpose of understanding this is so that you can be aware of what is and what is not dimming your communication with Heaven.

You can be completely clear minded, healthy, and doing all the right things to ensure you have crystal clear communication, but you still feel like you're receiving nothing or that you're being ignored. There is no such thing as Heaven overlooking you. When you feel you're being ignored, then something surrounding you is blocking the communication. When you push to receive a message from Heaven, then the communication is driven further away from you. Pushing for a message shoves it away. The pushing and hoping to make a connection blocks it because there is this anxious, nervous, frustrated, worry energy within. This can be where deep inside you feel you're not going to make that connection. If you're anxious to make a connection with your Spirit team, then this blocks it since it lowers your vibration. A low vibration is the equivalent to cutting off ones oxygen supply to breathe.

Your Clair channels are telecommunication receptors you use to communicate with your guides, angels, and any in Heaven with. Your various senses are the phone lines to your Spirit team. Everyone was born with sharp senses, which open and close throughout the duration of your life depending on your lifestyle choices, surroundings, thoughts, and feelings. When your Clair channels are free of toxic debris, then the clearer the messages and guidance is that comes in.

Your psychic abilities never go away even if it sometimes feels that way. They are under the surface and always accessible. When you don't feel psychic, it just means something is blocking it. Blocks can be certain foods, drinks, negative moods, bad energy, technological distractions, and other people. The closer you are to the physical Earth and nature, the easier it can be re-awakened. This means anything that is not manmade.

Some are drawn to the spiritual genre because they're interested in fortune telling. They're fixated on telling the future. Some do not want to know the future, while others are desperate to know the future. You want to know the future when you're in a place in your life that does not make you happy. Your dreams have not been realized, or when it comes to relationships and you have been single for quite some time, you wonder if you'll ever meet 'the one'. This isn't about being more psychic so that you can predict yours and others future. Much of the time related future predictions are difficult to assess since the mass majority operate on free will choice above Heaven's guidance. This is shifting and altering ones course dramatically every so often. Being more psychic here is to help you make better choices in your life. It's to help ensure that you stay on the right path. It's to bring you a healthier and happier existence.

Removing toxins in your life assists in opening up your Clair channels wider. There will be negativity that enters your vicinity, but when you're aware of when it happens, you're able to quickly take steps to modify it and bring you back to that centered space. This is why Heaven advises that you take care of yourself as best as you can. They might guide someone to be alcohol free, since they believe that no one needs any toxic vice if they're governing their life from a place of joy, love, and peace. The high that comes with those traits are beyond what any addiction can satisfy. In the end, moderation is important with anything and you're not going to Hell if you enjoy a glass of wine every night. They're merely explaining that it can block and dim the messages coming in. Toxins are not craved on a regular basis when someone is operating from a high vibration.

In order to be creative, you need to have focus, stamina, energy, motivation, and inspiration. When you've been feeling sluggish for days and don't know why, ask your team for help to give you natural energy. You can ask them to guide you to healthy products or to give you the steps you need to take to regain your strength. They may give you a simple task that is telling you to go to the gym for an hour. After you do that, you leave the gym as if you're floating on air with natural energy.

A successful working Medium friend who assists with solving crime cases informed me privately that she would have one beer or two before she begins filming an episode on television since it relaxes her. She will not have any more than that because then she'll just be all over the place and way too buzzed to connect.

What works for one person will not always work for

91

another. What is advised is a generality from my Spirit team who speaks on behalf of all in Heaven. They also reside and operate from a space that is challenging for the ego to get to. For that matter, they understand the struggles that human souls go through, but they feel that if everyone on the planet operated from the space they do, then there would be peace on Earth and toxic addictions wouldn't be desired. Everyone would be happy because no one is treating others disrespectfully or clawing their way to achieve or dominate. If everyone paid attention to Heaven, then love would reign. Unfortunately, this is not the world that exists today and human beings are to blame for that design.

You have the ultimate say on what works for you. This is your life and you must live it for you and do what you feel is best. When someone who loves to cook becomes accustomed to how to follow a new cooking recipe, they start to alter it a bit and add things here and take away things there. My team relays a structure for you to jump off of. When they make recommendations to watch what you ingest from unhealthy foods, to drugs, to alcohol, then it is for various reasons that include helping you be a stronger conduit with Heaven and to move your life into a happier content place.

When you focus on a health issue, you give more energy and power to it. This expands and makes it worse, which is what you want to avoid. There will be health issues you might be faced with. Understand that your soul is separate from what's happening to your physical body. Avoid labeling and identifying with a health issue. Believe everything will work out in the way that it's intended to. In the end, your soul is always intact regardless of what is happening to the physical body you temporarily inhabit.

YOU ARE WHAT YOU CONSUME

The FDA *(Food and Drug Administration)* is indirectly responsible for the premature deaths of many human souls due to their abusive power and control on potentially lifesaving products that are considered illegal in some areas. They are deciding what they think should be approved and what you should or should not ingest in your own body. They are human beings and human beings are flawed. It is no one's place to decide how you choose to live your life pending it isn't harming anyone. The government regulating what others should or should not have needs to be equipped with spiritually based people who have a stronger connection with God and therefore will know what would be good or not.

There is also an excess of human made drugs, foods, or drinks that are considered toxic to your body when taken regularly or in large quantities. These products are ironically legal.

Some see an issue with marijuana, but they have no issue with alcohol, which is responsible for more accidents, deaths, and harm on other people than weed. The only reason some find an issue with marijuana is because they were taught that it's a drug that is illegal, when in fact it's a plant that comes from the ground long before humankind existed. It is only illegal because human ego made it this way for various reasons. Because the government made alcohol legal, this is stuck in the minds of the human condition that it must be better than weed, since weed has a negative illegal undertone to it. It is only illegal in places because mankind chose to make it illegal. People are afraid of the word *illegal*, but something is only illegal, because mankind made it that way. It doesn't mean they are always right. They are flawed human beings making decisions for you. And in fact, over time things that were legal were made illegal and vice versa as they later discovered they made an error in judgment. Examine all of the atrocities and destruction created out of the choices humankind thought to be correct in the past and you get a pretty good observation into how you are controlled.

This isn't advocating that you smoke weed or drink alcohol. This is illustrating the way human souls perceive things around them. Most of it can be connected to the way they were taught. If you started out on Earth alone with no one else telling you what to do, what to eat, what to drink, then it would be interesting to note how you view your surroundings.

I have had others ask, "What do the angels say about eating meat?" They say, "No good."

I'm not a vegetarian, but I am fairly strict about what I consume to an extent, so I've asked for clarification and to expand. They went into that when you eat certain meat or anything that was a living soul, then you are eating that life force. The conditions of animals today in the way they turn them into food is horrific. You're eating their trauma. They're showing me crammed cages in abusive environments. They also explained that it's not a sin to eat meat. They mean it's no good for the human's health long term. There are exceptions such as if someone is eating meat that is organic, or where the animals are raised for food in loving conditions. There are certified organic farmland where no added growth hormones, pesticides, or antibiotics are used. Things are slowly changing since you can find these products in the stores now. The animals, plants, sea life, and all of that were partly put on Earth for human's survival. Humankind cannot survive necessarily by eating the leaf off a tree.

No one knows how an animal they're eating was raised. You're not going to Hell if you crave and eat a hot dog at a Carnival. Nor is someone who is a carnivorous eater their entire life going to be sent to Hell and damnation. Like anything that could potentially be toxic, meat should be consumed in moderation. The point is that caution should be adhered. Ultimately, you make the life choices that feel right to you.

There are many human souls sent here to battle the food corporations to get them to make their products naturally or organically. They are also fighting to get food companies to reveal what the product is made of on the label. It is interesting that some of the food companies are fighting right back to avoid having to do that. If what you're using is good, then you'll be proud to show that to the world on a label.

At this time a company called Monsanto is a big deal now since they are one of the largest organizations to use genetically engineered or modified seeds in their crops. This is otherwise known as GMO or Genetically Modified Organism. When human tampering starts genetically altering anything with chemicals, then you can guess what negative cons will come out of that.

One of the many issues that came out of that was the genetically modified soybean. It first came to light in the early 1990's. The soybean is toxic to human health especially in Men. It drops their testosterone levels at an earlier age than it's supposed to and raises the estrogen levels. Estrogen is great in high amounts in the female body, but not the male composition. Examine the male species post 1995 and how they differ in comparison to those of pre-early 1990's. The bottom line is some of the food companies use chemicals that have a high level of toxicity when consumed. Most people are consuming it and not aware of the buildup happening in their body over time.

Food corporations make so many products with all of these additives that are bad for you and create toxic build up in your system. Some will deny this and say that they have to make it this way to preserve the food. This food didn't exist centuries ago and humankind thrived and survived just fine.

The food companies and corporations often make products with all sorts of dangerous additives and ingredients that no one can pronounce or say. These products become addictive because they artificially alter that person's state of mind or mood temporarily into a feeling of joy. The human soul has been unable to replicate the kind of euphoric high they felt when back home in Heaven. It is challenging for them to get back to that state when they were a soul before they entered a human body. Therefore they consume human made products to get there. They become attracted to other addictions to fulfill a hole of loneliness, boredom, depression, or any other emotional state. This is what emotional eating is.

FALLING INTO ADDICTIONS

Some of the world's most successful people are goal oriented. They take action and go after what they want even when others tell them they have no business doing something. They pay no mind and continue to work at achieving their goals one after the other. You rarely hear about them succumbing to an addiction such as drugs, alcohol, or bad food. The only addiction they might be guilty of is one of winning and accomplishing. They're too busy to fall into a depression or time waster. When you're doing work that gives you pleasure, then this raises your vibration. The vibration rises above depression and toxic addictions. You no longer crave those substances because you're high on life.

While disciplined individuals can reach this heavenly euphoric state naturally through spiritual practices, it is still a struggle for human souls to achieve overall in the practical Earth world. The rebuttal or a non-believer might say something like, "You take care of yourself and live nine more miserable years longer than I do."

It is a myth to assume that someone who is regimented and takes care of oneself is unhappy. Someone who falls into the bell jar consuming an excess of human made addictions is typically the unhappy camper. Someone who is on cloud nine and feeling a natural love from within rarely craves a toxic addiction. I know what this is like since I've resided in both ends of the spectrum bouncing back and forth experiencing all of it.

I was involved in a love relationship in the past with someone who had an alcohol addiction, but craved the alcohol less while with me due to the natural feelings of love that were growing within while around me. When our connection dissolved, you can accurately guess that the craving for high amounts of alcohol rose up once again.

When you're in a healthy long term relationship, then that reduces or zaps away the desire to consume negative toxins and addictions in high quantities. The reason is love raises your vibration. When your vibration is high, then you don't crave or desire toxins. You are also less addicted to those substances. If you're someone battling addictions to something, it is often likely you'll fall back into that path while in this healthy loving long term relationship. This is because the love relationship can only sustain for so long before it is no longer in the newness category. An addicted person may grow bored or start to feel inadequate while in the love connection. They soon reach for the addiction in hopes it will remove those negative feelings. For some, they may fall into that addictive behavior, but they're absolved in it far less than when they're single and unhappy.

You are not being criticized if you have an addiction to particular toxic substances and obsessions. I am a lifelong addict and know firsthand what it's like to have an addiction to alcohol, drugs, vices, cigarettes, and sex. You name it and I probably did it. Ironically food was the only substance I've never had an addiction for. With the assistance of my Spirit team over the course of my life I diminished the harder addictions while in my twenties. I became more of a disciplined bloke who worked day in and day out to make it through without succumbing to the addiction as best I could. I've fallen into the addictive behavior from time to time, but hopped out just as quickly, whereas in my twenties I climbed in and stayed in. I'm what some might call a dry addict. This is someone who is not using addictions, but still behaving like an addict. Moderation or elimination is the better alternative in avoiding the dangers of toxic addictions.

Addictions break apart positive connections with others. They bring on an array of diseases and even premature death. In large quantities, they block and dim the connection with your Spirit team on the other side.

When you're in tune and connected to what's beyond, your life gradually begins to improve. When you're in tune to the guidance filtering through you from your Spirit team, you make fewer mistakes. You pick up on the Heavenly guidance that might be guiding you to your dream job, or to a loving soul mate partnership, to the right car, home, roads to take, and so forth. Being in tune elevates your life in a brighter way. It raises your vibration, which is the space where you are experiencing feelings of love, joy, and peace naturally.

DETOXIFY YOUR SOUL

How do you generally feel when you head off to bed every night? How is this feeling carried throughout the next day? What is the energy of the words that pass through your mind as that happens? Is it joyful, stressful, positive, negative, or full of sadness? What is your life like? Do you wake up in the morning and wonder what the point of getting up is? Or do you wake up and feel awesome ready to jump into the day with excitement? How long does that feeling last before you reach for something to give you a lift? What or who causes the feelings to drop? What can you do to change that? What about your thoughts? Are you generally a happy optimistic person or a down feeling kind of soul?

Many factors in your life will dictate the state of mind you will be in everyday. If you're someone who desires a loving partnership with someone and it has been years since that's happened, then you will move about each day with some despondence. Even when convinced you're enjoying life and you love your job, but then you head home and realize that you're single and there isn't anyone there to share your life with when you arrive. Maybe you live with a family member or you have a roommate. Those you live with can be a temporary distraction until you realize, "Oh wow, ten years have passed and I don't have a lover."

Perhaps you despise your job, but you're afraid to leave. You worry that you won't find another job and you have bills to pay. Human physical desires convert into toxins that buildup within your soul and this subsequently affects your physical body. It can leave you feeling consistently rundown. This is why it's crucial to detoxify and cleanse your body and soul as often as you can.

If you're a busy professional always working, then this is especially important. These toxins can also build up if you're unemployed, or if you're someone who lounges around the house all day bored with nothing around that excites you. The boredom feeling is what contributes to soul toxic build up. The fear energy of how bills will be paid when you're unemployed or if you will find another job can build up too.

I've had others approach me protesting that they've been drinking non-stop for days and need to stop. The great feeling they had when they started is no longer there. It no longer matters how much they drink because it is not helping. It's weighing them down causing them to feel agitated, lethargic, and unmotivated. You have one to two beers and you get a buzz. You start pounding back additional beers and you start to feel out of it. The negative health risks also increase if this is a regular habit.

Pay attention to what you put into your body. Utilize self-control if you've been on a killer streak of consuming toxins in high quantities. When you experience negative feelings or you're super sensitive, you reach for a toxic vice. This is more than just having a beer or a glass of wine. It's drinking a six pack or an entire bottle of wine. You feel high for about an hour or two, and then you start to come down from that and the feeling is much worse than before you had the drinks. You feel lethargic and it messes with your sleep. You wake up the next day feeling even more gross and sluggish. You count down the hours in the day before you can have another drink again just to make it all go away. Days have gone by and nothing has been accomplished, and not to mention that you've been unhappy throughout the whole process.

The super sensitive of the world are more in tune and connected than they might realize. You have a greater frequency of psychic reception than others do. Make lifestyle adjustments that are more conducive to your sensitivity levels. This is by being cautious with who you connect, communicate, or hang out with. Follow your gut if you're not feeling like going to a social event you've been invited to. Pick and choose which events you go to and what has the greater benefit to your overall well-being.

A positive way to deal with moodiness, sensitivity, or a rise in negative feelings is to dive into a creative project. Negative feelings are a sign that your soul is starving to create. It's a great way to unleash and release all of that built up negativity.

When a popular artist in entertainment culture experiences a painful relationship break up, in the end they ultimately channel that pain into writing songs and making another record. Actors find characters to play that might be the opposite of who they are in order to release any repression and emotional toxins. You don't have to necessarily try to be an actor in films or a singer on stage, but you can take an acting class for the fun of it. You can find positive creative outlets to unleash your downward spiral of emotions. With the way technology is accessible today, you can film your own acting pieces or record it into a microphone even if it's just for your eyes and ears only.

There are times where nothing specific happened to contribute to mood decline. It is the result of a physically inherited genetic disposition. Other times something happened in your life that upset your world. The third way is that the mood decline is a result of what you're ingesting, be it food, pills, drugs, alcohol, etc. You could be eating something that you love, but happens to be high in sugar. It lifts you up only to drop you down to the floor an hour or so later. Keep an eye on what you put into your body regularly and test products out to assess what could be triggering a sudden mood drop. Do a daily test by examining and testing out what products you consume that could be the cause of regular lethargy or negative moods. The most obvious causes are alcohol or drugs, but sometimes it's food you wouldn't think to be the cause of. It can be dairy, too much caffeine, red meat, or the supplements you take.

CARING FOR YOUR SKIN

When I see the human skin, clairvoyantly it appears to be covered with little cell like mouths all over every inch of your body. It breathes in the pollutants in the air, sucks in the energy of other people, and becomes clogged and closed up whenever any form of toxins hit it. Your skin craves the thirst from touch. It inhales the vibrations in its surroundings. Taking care of your skin and your body as much as possible is vital and beneficial. This means checking out the kinds of soaps, shampoos, and lotions you use to ensure they're not damaging. Some use natural essential oils, which are derived from plants. When anything touches your skin, then these cells drink all of that in. Ensure that what you're putting on your skin isn't toxic. Archangel Raphael says that if it is toxic, then it is the equivalent to someone drinking bleach.

Touch awakens these mouths over the skin. This can be through a lovers or friends touch, or by the hands of a masseuse. Masseuse here means anyone who knows how to massage someone else whether it is a friend or lover. I've seen little kids playing around and massaging their mother's shoulders for fun after a long day at work. This is beyond a massage therapist, even though a professional massage therapist is ideal.

The topic of tattoos has been brought up with me as well. Getting tattoos is a personal choice. I'm surrounded by family members and siblings covered in tattoos. I'm no stranger to it and attract those who are big on self-expression into my world. Tattoos are creative attributes that express ones individualism. There are risks involved with tattoos, such as injecting ink into your skin, which can cause an infection due to bad needles. There is no denying that puncturing the skin is going to have some measure of effect, but it isn't going to kill you. A needle is puncturing into the skin and depositing ink. There are other parts of one's body that is not tattooed that has just enough visible mouths for it to not be a problem. When one chooses to get tattooed, they should take precautions such as making sure the needles are sterilized and the ink being used is only for them and no one else. It should be looked upon that the work area is as clean and hygienic as anything else in your world.

If anything is touching your skin, you want to make sure it's not toxic. This includes the clothes you wear too. Some fabrics are made in toxic chemicals that touch your skin. Even washing it before you wear it might not always help. And there are some laundry detergents that can be filled with toxins and chemicals, which cause you to break out. They can produce an allergic reaction after you put the clothes on after the wash. You'll want to be mindful of the soaps you use to wash your clothes too.

For women, certain underwear can cause an issue such as thongs, which can contribute to a urinary tract infection or vaginal problems. Certain tight underwear might be sexy, but if that's all you're wearing it can harbor bacteria. High heels are damaging to a woman's feet if that's all you mostly wear as well as constricting tight outfits.

For men, wear boxers more than underwear briefs. The male testes are outside of the body for a reason. It needs to move freely and not be restricted. There are exceptions at times such as if one is playing sports or being physically active, then it needs to be protected, but if you're sitting down all day, then wear boxers. This is more of a guideline of how often one wears boxers as opposed to constricting underwear. Underwear drops the male sperm count and it can take two to three months to reproduce and increase it.

Wear that sexy underwear or those hot outfits, but in moderation to avoid potential long-term health issues.

GUILTY PLEASURES

Pray for assistance and intervention daily to be led to the right products that will not be damaging to your body. The obvious toxic culprits are vices or guilty pleasures like alcohol, drugs, nicotine, sugar, salt, fatty foods, and high amounts of caffeine. No one is going to reprimand you for eating a hamburger, unless it's a Vegetarian activist who sneers whenever you eat meat in front of them. The reason the angels are always preaching about avoiding toxins when possible is for your benefit. They know that consuming toxic products in high quantities will block the communication with them. This also contributes to you missing out on beneficial instructions given to you in order to achieve your desires.

Toxins are a breeding ground for harder health issues down the line. These products also dictate how you will feel. There will be an initial high the toxin gives you, but then it is soon reversed shooting you to the floor. It weighs you down and makes you sluggish, depressed, irritable, and so forth. Who wants to feel that way day in and day out? You reach for the toxin again to get that temporary high. Multiply that every day and visualize what that could possibly be doing to your insides and your aura. You might not think so or care at age twenty-three, but come sixty-three, you'll be wishing you had done things a little differently in your life.

Caffeine and alcohol are two of the top toxins that human souls consume and abuse more than any other. These are also toxins that the angels feel that no one needs if you structure your life in a way where those cravings are limited or not desired. Can you blame the world though? Look at the kind of lives that human souls have created. It's been designed in a way that ensures people run themselves into the ground leaving them permanently exhausted, stressed, and dejected. It's a struggle for most to achieve profound happiness, so they reach for toxins in high quantities to help get through it.

You have some form of caffeine to get yourself going in the morning and you keep this momentum every few hours just to get through the day. When you're unhappy, this drains your life force energy leaving you feeling as if you need high doses of caffeine to feel energized. I've worked with executives in the past who drink soda all day long to keep them flying. This isn't one soda, but many throughout the day. Multiply doing that by two decades and imagine what will happen to you. No matter how much caffeine you have, you're still feeling the constant daily crash. If you overdo caffeine, then this can cause more stress and anxiety within you, not to mention the damage it does to your heart and health over time.

There was a case of a man who abused caffeine to the point where he was diagnosed with liver cancer.

Granted he admitted to drinking six to seven energy drinks a day and had a poor diet of pizza and burgers. This is far more excessive than the daily caffeine jolt. He passed away at the young age of thirty-nine.

If you're unable to quit a toxin right away or do not want to, work on reducing it so that you're indulging it in moderation. Moderation is having an alcoholic drink or a cup of coffee once a day, rather than drinking it until you drop. It's what it's doing to you or will do to you down the line if you're consuming large quantities of it daily. Reducing your toxin intake and balancing it with healthy stuff is a great step in the right direction to being happier, healthier, and more connected with the other side.

Let's say that you're unable to quit having a couple cups of coffee to get going in the morning, but you know you want to. Adopt a balance with some carrot juice, herbal teas, or tons of water preceding that as your day continues on.

Incorporate a detoxifying cleanse every so often. This can be where one day you shut off all technological distractions or time wasters. If that's impossible or difficult, then start small where it's shut off for several hours or your personal cell phone is off during your entire workday. Use your sound judgment on when it's practical to do so. You do not want to vanish for days on end when there is an emergency, crises, or even death in your life and no one can find you. The technological detox can include spending this day away from stressful and drama filled people. Consume high vibration food into your system such as fruits and vegetables. Notice how you feel when you do this and compare it to those days where you're taking a pound of sugar in your coffee.

More people lead sedentary lives than ever before. You're either parked all day on your rear at an office job, standing behind a register, or plopped in a chair at home with little to no movement for hours on end. Over time this begins to increase the risks of health related issues, not to mention your energy levels permanently drop and your body begins to feel as if it's eternally out of whack. Incorporate regular exercise at least once a day if possible. Take frequent walks, jog, or bike when you're able to. If you're suffering from a physical issue that makes exercise difficult, then add in certain exercises that are safe to keep the blood flow moving. When unsure of what you can handle or what is good for you, then talk to a medical or professional licensed expert when incorporating health, fitness, and nutrition related action steps into your life.

Regular exercise is one of the bigger guidance and messages I've received and have been preaching about longer than anything else. Treating the temporary vessel you're renting with the utmost compassion and care is always urged. If you poured something other than gasoline into your car, it would tear your car up. Treat your body the way you would a car to ensure optimum performance.

Archangel Raphael is the healing angel to call on for assistance with all health and well being related issues. Ask Raphael or your Spirit team to help in reducing your cravings for toxic vices, or to eliminate it knowing deep down that you're ready. Your team will work with you on that after you have made a specific request to begin the process of reducing or eliminating something you're trying to control. Request to be guided to healthier alternatives and to incorporate a more balanced intake.

FRESH AIR AND WATER

Fresh air is one of the most important elements to awaken your psychic gifts. This is because spirit power is heavy outdoors. The messages from Heaven travel through the molecules of oxygen. Get out there in nature, amongst the trees, grass, flowers, sunshine, and take deep healthy breaths in. Open your windows at home daily allowing the fresh oxygenated air to flow in clearing out all of the toxins that build up in a home with the windows permanently shut. Fresh air means clean air, not smog polluted air.

Many human souls get up every morning five days a week to sit in an enclosed car to go to an enclosed office to sit in all day. They hardly go outside for their breaks. At the end of the day they climb back into their enclosed car, to go to their enclosed home, and then repeat the next day. Many cities have built shopping malls, theater complexes, promenades, apartment complexes, and grocery stores on top of one another. It's grown to become void of quiet nature settings. Land developers don't care about trees. They care about building, which isn't a problem until you're building shamelessly and unwisely on top of one another.

Take steps to include more fresh air in your life. Make a pact to take breaks throughout the day where you can get outside and at least walk around the block.

When you arrive back home, open all of your windows, and allow the fresh air to waft in if even for a few minutes. Go for walks after dinner, or get in a work out before dinner. Get plenty of exercise and fresh air. These are two key secrets to integrate into your life in order to awaken the creative part of you. This also cracks open your psychic gifts that every soul was born with while strengthening your health and overall well-being.

Water governs so much of this planet from the ocean, to the lakes, to the human body. Water is one of the most awesome detoxifiers! This includes bathing, swimming, or sitting in front of an ocean or lake if you're near one. If you're not, then the power of visualization can take you there. Open up ocean photographs on your computer or thumb through a photography book of beaches and meditate on them. Drink plenty of water every day to flush out the toxins in your body.

The world's oceans are critical to human survival and its habitat. It must be kept clean of toxins the same way you keep your physical body clear of toxins. The ocean is what contributes to the clouds that form in the sky, which produces the water your body needs in order to endure life in a healthier way. When one heads to a non-crowded beach they have reported to feeling more relaxed and alive than they did before they went to the beach. Those who live along the coast have been reported to have stronger health than others might. The ocean breeze blows away smog particles that the rest of a big city would breathe in. It increases your body's ability to absorb oxygen. If you're not near an ocean, or lake, then the water comes to you by drinking it, taking a shower, bath, or through the power of visualization. The mind is a powerful device and can take you anywhere you want to go and bring you anything you desire including what you do not desire, so use it wisely.

Chapter Eleven

Battling Illnesses

*M*ental Health issues affect millions of people around the world. The general list includes depression, anxiety, and the various ailments from eating disorders, to psychotic and mood disorders. Those suffering from some form of mental health issues find that it prevents them from living the kind of life they dream of. It can prevent you from going after what you want or inhibit you from defending yourself. For some it can lead to suicide or permanent stagnancy.

Depression sufferers feel inadequate or unable to motivate themselves to live. Agoraphobics are afraid to leave their homes, or they feel uncomfortable in crowded places, or confined spaces. Those with social anxiety avoid accepting invitations to parties or functions, as they fear being watched, judged, or simply cannot handle the huge amount of psychic stimuli tampering their system. As you get to know others on a personal level, there isn't anyone who isn't battling some form of disorder or phobia connected to ones mental health. You might never fully diminish them in one lifetime, but you can get pretty close to where you're able to function somewhat realistically in this hostile world.

Almost everyone on the planet has some sort of neurosis, while others may battle harder versions of these disorders. Some of these disorders are genetic and inherited. They run right down the genetic blood line. Other times it's taught or placed on the back of that soul. Many struggle with disorders their entire life or attempt to temper it and keep it under control.

For those who battle disorders, it might please you to know that some of the most successful people in the world battle some of these same issues. Entertainers from well known actors to singers wrestle with social anxiety. They are able to train themselves to shut it off temporarily when they are in the performing zone, whether on stage or in front of the camera. Some are born into this life with it, while others develop it over the duration of their Earthly life.

Due to the rise of technology, selfies, and phones, narcissism is a trait that is grown and bred into the generations raised post 1995. From that point forward, Earth's history moved into a generation being raised on technology, selfies, and computers. This has rendered many incapable of carrying in person conversations or exuding proper class etiquette. Many are growing up in environments where they are assaulted by selfishness in others every second. You cannot hide from it or be unaware of it unless you live in the middle of nowhere and never go online. This along with poor diet and nutrition all contribute to the high amounts of anxiety, depression, and mental health issues that exist.

Some choose to take anti-depressants or anti-anxiety medication, while others refuse to as they feel that it alters their brain chemistry artificially. They prefer to engage in counseling with a therapist or talk therapy instead, while others participate in counseling along with medication. These are choices that are up to you and your doctor. It's your life and you know what's best for you to get through it. Ironically, I've discovered those that are against medication, seem to self-medicate in other ways that are not exactly healthy.

Those suffering from social anxiety know what it's like to have their thoughts, feelings, and heart racing for no apparent reason. Someone is walking towards you to talk to you, and you want to jump out of your skin. You want them to go away. You don't want to have to talk to them, deal with people, stand up, and give a speech, and so forth. You desire a daily pill to keep those issues contained as much as possible. Do what you feel is best for you. There is nothing wrong with wanting to be on medication or wanting to dissolve medication. This is a personal choice that you make. With anything health related, always seek out a professional medical doctor regardless of what anyone states. Take hold of the reigns and govern your life the way you see fit.

Schizophrenia goes away when the soul crosses over as all mental issues do. Someone with schizophrenia can take medication to mask the symptoms, or they adjust their lifestyle and way of living to help it be more manageable. This is the same way anyone who suffers from any form of mental disorder this lifetime. If you have social anxiety, then you don't spend your days heading to areas that are jam packed with people. If you go to an amusement park, then you go on a day that you know isn't so crowded. You avoid going to the grocery store at high noon on a weekend when it's typically more packed than at any other hour.

Efficient ways of eliminating a toxic addiction such as bad foods, drugs, alcohol, cigarettes, caffeine, or coffee is by gradually reducing it over time.

I understand the day to day struggles that exist in life as I've been through those trenches too. I know how to navigate through it. I've been in the gutters of addiction as I have an addictive personality, but I also have a strong connection with the other side. I've learned from Heaven that the only person beating up on you is *you*. Everyone has their own gauge on what works for them. It's about doing the best you can. If you fall off the wagon, you don't beat yourself up. You get back on the horse again and continue moving forward one day at a time.

Hyper focus on anything expands whatever the attention is on. If it's focused on a health concern, the healing takes longer to come about. Great health improvements are made through prayer and by shifting your focus positively away from the issue. I've had catastrophic health issues that were painful, but went away after I believed it would improve and get better. Instead, I focused on fun, joy, laughter, and did whatever I could to get to that place from watching a funny movie to joking around with a pal.

There are shattering health issues that do or will come about that are beyond human and Heaven's control. It's better to look upon it with positive thoughts, rather than negative. The negative thoughts will only make you feel that much worse. At least the positive thoughts will ensure you remain in high spirits throughout the process.

I've had major health scares in the past that were physically painful, but I continued to ask for help and eventually one day it was no more. It was as if it never happened. I have days where I'm not focused or my faith is waning, but I quickly revert back to being focused not long afterwards.

I haven't had the full-blown flu since the early 2000's. I should add right here, "Knock on wood." When you work on taking care of yourself regularly and treat what you put into your body with the utmost care, then any illnesses that arise are minimal. I've certainly felt worn down as if I was coming down with something, but as soon as I'm aware of that, I immediately up my preventatives before it blows up. I wake up the next day feeling great again. When I feel my body under stress and my immune system declining, I'm guided to begin my remedies to get better quickly. I immediately double the water and vitamin C intake. I sleep earlier and longer than usual while avoiding strenuous exercise or anything that can cause anxiety. I may do wheatgrass and blue algae shots as well as making sure I'm relaxed and detached from any stress.

Exceptions to this are you may be an older person or younger unhealthy person where it takes longer for your body to fight off illnesses. There are also circumstances where you discover it was beyond your control.

When you feel a cold or the flu coming on, immediately start the regimen. Drink lots of water and up the Vitamin C intake. You can go as far as to drink a shot or two of wheatgrass if you can keep it down. Above all you must sleep more than you usually do.

When your body is wearing down, this is a sign that you need to take it easy and rest. If you watch movies, then stick to comedies, since lightheartedness, joy, and laughter raise your vibration. When you're sick or your immune system is crashing, then your vibration is low. This will help raise it and help you get better quicker!

Avoid strenuous exercises during this time so as not to wear your body out and dehydrate it. Although some exercise is helpful such as casual biking or walking, but you won't do that when you have the full blown flu.

Drink more water than usual. If you drink 50 ounces a day, then aim for 100 ounces. Head to bed earlier than you normally would. Sleep, water, and prayer will rejuvenate your body quickly.

Other preventatives might include water with squeezed lemon or lime, and a dash of cayenne pepper. Add a healthy sweetener, or agave syrup if it's too difficult to take down. Heat it up and then drink. Other flu and cold illness fighting preventatives that are high in Vitamin C are jalapeno peppers, onions, algae, and garlic.

Archangel Raphael is the healing angel to call on for all things healing, health, nutrition, exercise, and well-being related.

Chapter Twelve

The Chakras

A Chakra *(pronounced "shock-ruh")* is an energy point within your soul's aura. There are hundreds of chakras throughout the soul and body, but there are eight core chakras that dominate. Your chakra is where God, your life force, and energy flow through. Each chakra looks like a colored spinning wheel to a clairvoyant or someone who has the ability to see the colors of one's aura. They see the individual chakra's spinning like little fans located at specific points of the body from head to toe.

Each chakra emits a different color. They spin counter clockwise and look like an oscillator fan emitting a different color out of it. When the color grows dirty, dark, or muddy, then this can indicate a problem in that area. When you experience anything negative related to what that chakra represents, then this dulls the color of the fan and changes the size of the chakra. It doesn't matter what size the chakra is. What is important is that all the chakras be relatively the same size. When one or more of the chakras are a different size than the others, then this can suggest an imbalance in a specific part of your life.

The chakras are not physical in nature, meaning it's not a human organ or something that is detectable to the human eye. The knowledge of chakras started out as a belief system in India that was eventually adopted worldwide in many spiritual or new age circles.

Each chakra represents a part of you and your life. The first three chakras are located from the pelvic area to just below the rib cage. Those chakras spin slowly representing physical external issues and circumstances. They emit a brighter joyful warmer color from red, orange, and yellow. The remaining five core chakras are located from the chest up through the top of your head. Those chakras spin much faster than the other three and represent more personal issues and circumstances. They emit a more subdued calming color from green, light blue, maroon, indigo, and violet.

Each of the core eight chakras spins quicker than the chakra below it. For example, the root chakra at the base spins slowly, while the sacral chakra above it spins slightly faster than the root chakra, and so forth.

When you negatively focus on a particular issue in your life, then this can imply that the chakra that represents the issue is dirty and off balance. When you have a dirty chakra, then this can compound the issues associated with that chakra. It also creates unevenness in your world while blocking the communication line to Heaven. This is why it's beneficial to touch on the core individual chakras. This is for those who don't know much about it or what they represent. When your chakra energy points are clear of debris and spinning at optimum levels, then this gives you greater psychic perception and input. This assists in awakening the creative spirit part of you.

In this chapter, we will briefly look at the eight core chakras starting at the bottom and moving our way up to the top so that you have a basic idea of what they represent.

Root Chakra – Red

The Root Chakra sits at the base of your spine. The root is like the root or base of a tree. When properly nourished, the roots come up from the ground and blossom into a tree, plant, or flower. The root chakra concept is much like the growth of a plant. When you nurture and take care of it, then this adds nourishment to the other chakras helping them strengthen. It is closest to the Earth and therefore connected to all things related to earthly issues and needs. This means that concerns surrounding money, security, physical desires, and wishes are all connected to the root chakra.

When you have money issues or worry about paying your bills, or you have concerns connected to your physical possessions such as your car or any material items, then this dirties up your root chakra. This also includes concerns having to do with your career and work related circumstances. If you do not feel appreciated at work, or you don't make enough money, or you have any sort of fear connected to work, career, or life purpose, then this will create an imbalance in the root chakra area.

The root chakra spins with an illumination of the color red. The stronger the red, the more activated the chakra is. When it is less activated, the color is a muddier red and the wheel putters and attempts to poorly spin around. It's like a clogged fan having a difficult time getting started.

The root chakra is connected to your physical desires. It is at the base of your spine and represents your desires for a secure firm foundation in your life. In order for a tree to grow and blossom, it must first have strong roots firmly implanted into the ground. When this is set, it begins to grow and prosper. This same concept is how the chakra's work. Ground and stabilize your root chakra, then this will help feed the other chakras.

Other signs your root chakra is unstable are when you experience fear and anxiety about your future or over anything that knocks your secure stability off kilter. When you roam through life feeling anxiety, insecure, or unsafe, then this is a sign your root chakra is dirty. Anxiety of any kind is connected to fear. Fear is connected to the root chakra. Symptoms can be chronic laziness, fatigue, anxiety, depression, anger, or irritability.

Signs that you have a strong root chakra are when you feel confident, stable, and grounded. Physical exercise or activity can help strengthen your root chakra. Keeping your body strong is of benefit to your root chakra and your overall health. Removing negative feelings of fear or insecurity in areas connected to your physical survival clears up any gunk in your root chakra. Get out in nature and plant your feet on the physical Earth to ground and stabilize your body and soul, which brightens up your root chakra.

Archangel Michael is the being to call on to assist in strengthening your root chakra. He can extract fear and insecurities from your aura and boost your confidence and optimism.

Sacral Chakra – Orange

The Sacral Chakra is the second chakra located in the pelvic/reproductive area below the navel and slightly above the Root Chakra. It glows a bright orange when spinning at a peak level.

The sacral chakra *(pronounced Say-Krull)* is connected to your passions, sensuality, and creativity. It is what brings you joy, pleasure, and enjoyment. When you express yourself creatively, then the cleaner your sacral chakra is. If you have a healthy sex drive, or the creative part of you is fully awakened, then you have a strong sacral chakra.

Someone with perpetual addictive behavior patterns is likely to have a dirty sacral chakra. There is a difference between a healthy sex drive and sex addiction. There is a distinction between enjoying a beer or two, and drinking a six-pack in one sitting. The enjoyment and pleasure of a glass of wine is beautiful as you soak in the valley of wine country on a hot Summer day. The opposite extreme is drinking a bottle of wine alone every night in your room to escape or push down your emotions. The addiction dirties up the sacral chakra.

Positive ways of clearing the sacral chakra are by immersing yourself into creative projects or a creative hobby. Other ways to brighten up your sacral chakra are by partaking in exercises and lifestyle choices that improve your overall well-being, emotional state, which also awaken your creative side.

The sacral chakra is also connected to your reproductive organs, not just sexually, but the organs themselves from a health and clinical perspective.

When your emotional equilibrium is all over the place and not in balance, then this can cause your sacral chakra to become clogged and dirty. You know this is the case if you find that your emotions are rising into co-dependency with anyone you come across whether it's a love relationship, friendship, or someone you're getting to know. Someone who lives for toxic drama and gossip have a muddy sacral chakra. Obsessions over food or gluttony lead to an unbalanced sacral chakra as well.

Activate your sacral chakra by partaking in activities that bring you joy and harmony. This is pending that it is not toxic or an addiction. Take a weekend getaway trip to somewhere amazing with a loved one. Spend that time connecting and having fun together. Kiss and make passionate love to one another. Dive into a creative project or hobby. All of this brightens up, activates, and awakens your sacral chakra

Bring your life and habits to the level of passion,

sensuality, joy, harmony, sexuality, and creativity in order to balance out your sacral chakra.

Archangel Jophiel and Archangel Gabriel are the higher beings to call on to assist in balancing your sacral chakra. They work by igniting your passion, sensuality, beauty, joy, and creativity essence.

Solar Plexus Chakra – Yellow

The Solar Plexus Chakra is the third Chakra located below the navel and above the Sacral Chakra. It glows a bright yellow like the Sun when it is spinning in top form. It is linked to your power and how you express yourself. Do you express yourself through aggressiveness, passive aggressiveness, or assertiveness? This is all connected to the solar plexus chakra, which is your inner power and willpower.

Having a strong solar plexus chakra is when you are centered and balanced. Someone who reacts dramatically or with hyper emotions to circumstances does not have a strong solar plexus at that moment. You have a strong solar plexus chakra when you have a clear mind about things. You think logically, openly, and methodically. You have great drive, persistence, and ambition. You're a go getter and ensure that business is taken care of. If you want something, you get to work on figuring out how to achieve it.

You know when your solar plexus chakra is becoming dirty when you exhibit feelings of low self-esteem, or when your emotions are perpetually on the negative side and all over the place. Loving, accepting, and appreciating all that you are gives you a clear clean running solar plexus chakra.

While someone with a strong solar plexus chakra will go after what they want and are ambitious, the flipside of that and what muddies up your solar plexus chakra is when you are controlling, domineering, and egotistical. This is also someone who bullies others online or in person. It's the negative commenter on any Internet story or page.

Having a weak solar plexus chakra is also if you live in denial around an issue. You have no will power or you give your power away to others. It's when you have obsessions of being powerful or the opposite extreme where you allow others to dominate you. This can also be in the work arena where you feel victim to a toxic co-worker or boss. The toxic co-worker or boss is being egotistical or narcissistic also, which dulls the solar plexus chakra.

Igniting your inner life force gives you a robust solar plexus chakra. It is standing strong in your power and having a durable sense of confident self. It is having integrity and exuding assertiveness with your dealings with others. It is being centered and focused on getting the job done without desire for a return.

Archangel Nathaniel and Archangel Ariel are the ones to call on to assist you with your solar plexus chakra. They work to help you stand in your power, have confidence, go after what you want, and to express yourself clearly with assertive compassion.

Heart Chakra – Green

The Heart Chakra is the fourth chakra located in

your physical heart and chest area. It is also in the middle of the eight core chakras blending both the physical and emotional/spiritual parts of you. It spins more rapidly than the previous three chakras illuminating a beautiful emerald green light.

As you might likely guess, the heart chakra is connected to all things having to do with love. This includes your love relationships and connections with others such as friendships, family members, acquaintances, and colleagues. If any of your connections are toxic or cause you ill will feelings, then this breaks your heart chakra.

An ex-lover has pulled a number on you leaving you saddened. You move through all of the various states of emotion from depression to anger to revenge. All of those states of emotion, while a natural reaction to having a love relationship end, also muddies up your heart chakra. This blocks love from coming in.

The heart chakra is connected to issues with all relationships from love, personal, business, to your negative states of emotion. When you cut off love and do not allow love in for fear of getting hurt or any other reason, then you clog up the heart chakra.

Ways to clean and clear the heart chakra is to remember to get back to that place where you can love again. When you forgive a partner you begin the process of cleaning the heart chakra. Perhaps they cheated on you or were abusive. Both of which are difficult to forgive or forget. Regardless, in order to clear the heart chakra of toxic debris, you must reach that place where you forgive them for yourself and your own benefit. You say, "What you did to me was not cool, but I forgive you so that I don't have to carry this pain anymore. And now I release you from my aura permanently."

The heart chakra is also connected to your Clairsentience Clair. Having a strong heart chakra awakens your Clairsentience. This is your psychic feeling sense. Activate your heart chakra by lifting your emotions and feelings to that of love, joy, and peace. This will bring on a crystal clear communication line with Heaven through Clairsentience.

Those with a strong heart chakra are warm, friendly, and open. They hold no judgment or criticism. Like the previous chakra, you can likely guess that all of those who think or post negative words and comments online have a dirty heart chakra as well.

Other ways to awaken your heart chakra are through having a healthy loving relationship, or by expressing kind words to those around you. Being supportive, loving, and partaking in self-care activates this chakra. Do things that give you a euphoric happy feeling of love, including watching a romantic comedy. Love all that you are inside and out. Love is the reason all are here and this is why having a beautiful radiating heart chakra is especially vital to your overall health and well-being.

Archangel Raphael, Archangel Haniel, or Archangel Chamuel are the hierarchy angels to call on to assist you with your heart chakra. They work with you on matters of love, healing, emotions, and attracting in high vibration connections.

Throat Chakra – Light Blue

The Throat Chakra is the fifth chakra and located in your throat. It spins faster than the previous chakras while illuminating a light blue or sky blue color. The throat chakra is the area you communicate and express your thoughts.   where you communicate.   This includes verbally, in writing, cell phone text, or social media.   Having a strong throat chakra is by expressing yourself clearly with compassion and without fear of censure.   When you censure yourself or hold your thoughts and feelings in, then this affects the functioning of your throat chakra.

The throat chakra is about speaking your truth. Writers, channelers, and speakers tend to have strong throat chakras when they're working, because they are getting everything that is stuck inside them and expressing it outwardly whether on a page or to an audience. This is pending they're writing and speaking the truth without fear of being judged, criticized, or censured.

Make note of how some of the previous chakras are connected to one another. When your sacral chakra is not expressing itself through creativity, or the solar plexus chakra is preventing you from being assertive, and your heart chakra is closed up, then this can prevent you from expressing yourself with communication through your throat chakra.

If you feel as if your throat chakra has been getting dirtier, then ways to clear and cleanse it requires communicating more vocally and truthfully without fear. This doesn't mean with anger or aggression, but with assertiveness and compassion. When you communicate in a hostile manner, such as attacking others, then that dims the auric filed around the throat chakra. It's just as bad if not worse as holding your thoughts inside because you're darting that energy at others and the universe. The damage has consequences since it reaches more targets. When you hold it inside, this only hurts yourself.

Practice journaling or writing down all the things that bother you. You can write it in a journal or in an email and send it to yourself. If you wished you could've said all the things that you were thinking when your ex decided to leave you, then write it out in an email to yourself or in a journal to get it out of you. Otherwise this will squelch and tighten up your throat chakra.

Singer entertainer Shania Twain has recounted losing her voice over the years. This was due to all of the hurt, anger, anxiety, and sadness she was experiencing as her first marriage crumbled. She did not express how she was feeling and this manifested into her losing the ability to sing. Eventually, she went through some spiritual healing and forgiveness steps in a therapeutic way that resulted in assisting in re-awakening her throat chakra. This is featured in a 6-episode series called, "Why Not? With Shania Twain." It was episode 4 that takes her through the transition into opening up her voice again, which I recommend watching.

When someone is unkind and you're unable to communicate that to them out of fear or any other reason, then write it in an email to yourself, to a friend, or in a journal. Write down everything you always wanted to say to them. You can speak as freely and as uncensored as you like since you most likely would not be sending it to them. The writing assignment is a great way to release toxins in your throat chakra while balancing it out and brightening it up.

All things having to do with communication are connected to your throat chakra. This includes speaking and communicating clearly with loved ones, friends, colleagues, acquaintances, and all you come across. Activate it by expressing your thoughts clearly and with compassion.

Archangel Gabriel is the one to call on to assist with your Throat Chakra. She helps with communicating on all levels.

Ear Chakra – Maroon

The Ear Chakra is the sixth chakra and located slightly above both of your ears. It illuminates the color of Maroon (or Red Violet). This chakra is sometimes disregarded or not typically mentioned, but it is equally important. The ear chakra is a chakra that exists and affects all things connected to your hearing. This is regardless if you were born deaf or not.

Your clairaudience clear hearing channel is located in your ear chakra. When one has a strong working ear chakra, the louder the voices of spirit and Heaven come in.

The ways that the ear chakra can become muddy are by absorbing negative words being spoken by someone else to you or another. Hearing these words moves through your ear chakra and creates dust particles on it. Hearing negative words also comes from those around you in conversation. You get into an elevator where two people are complaining about work to one another, then you are absorbing the negative energy of those words through your ear chakra. Negative entertainment media such as television programs, movies, or songs can also affect the ear chakra.

The connection you have with Heaven is exceptionally strong through the ear chakra. This means someone who has no belief in the other side will tend to have a dirtier ear chakra than one who has faith. Your negative thoughts travel through your ear chakra as well so you want to be careful if you're constantly bombarding your own consciousness with the negative words of your ego.

Ways to clear your ear chakra are through intention. Visualize the bright light of Heaven being filtered through this chakra and blasting away all debris. Avoid hanging around those who are perpetually negative or gossips. Also, shut out loud irritating noises on the street such as traffic, car sounds, honking, trash cans banging, sirens, etc. All of that filters into your ear chakra and muddies it up creating a block with your clairaudience. Be mindful of the television programs you watch as you're listening to that too. When you watch movies you enjoy that have harsh negative language, then be sure to separate that from reality. Create a shield or wall between yourself and the film.

The ear chakra is in constant connection with the throat chakra. When you hear someone say something to you, it moves through your ear chakra, then when you respond in kind, the words travel out through your throat chakra.

I was born with heightened Clairaudience that

ironically filters through one of my ears that was discovered to be deafer than the others when I was a kid. I was unable to pass any of the hearing tests with that ear. The irony is that the voices of my Spirit team filter loudly through that ear as if they're standing next to me.

The discs of the ear chakra are slightly above both ears and move in tandem with one another. If you hear negative words and absorb it in one ear, this affects both ear chakras at the same time. They equally receive dust particles in them in the same spot on both discs.

Archangel Zadkiel is the one to call on to assist with clearing out the toxins of your ear chakra and help you hear the voices of spirit more clearly.

Third Eye Chakra – Indigo

The Third Eye Chakra is the seventh chakra and located between your two physical eyes, but raised just slightly above it. It spins illuminating the color of Indigo. The third eye chakra is your psychic and spiritual perception. Having a strong third eye chakra equates to having a keen Clairvoyance channel, otherwise known as clear seeing. You receive visual impressions like a mini movie playing in front of you that has significance to you or someone else. It can be what's happened, what's to come, or what's coming up. Many equate the third eye chakra to being more psychic, but the truth is that having a balanced chakra system makes one a stronger conduit with spirit. You can be highly psychic by having a strong heart chakra since that is connected to Clairsentience, and yet your third eye chakra is dimmer than the others.

Because the Third Eye is what is unseen, most are not aware of it or thinking about it. This act in itself closes up the Third Eye. Signs that your third eye chakra is opening up are seeing violet sparkles everywhere, or you're able to see the eye sitting on its side staring back at you when you close your physical eyes. You might start to have vivid dreams or you constantly see etheric images put in front of you of what's to come. You see spirits as opaque or translucent around you. Someone who is afraid of seeing spirits will cause the third eye chakra to close up.

Like the ear chakra, when one is a non-believer of anything spiritual related then this causes the third eye chakra to become dirty and shut down. The third eye chakra is the eye or window that sees what others cannot see. It is the window into the other side, spirit worlds, and dimensions that exist. When you're able to see the Third Eye, you view it sitting on its side looking right at you from within your mind. This is different than the physical eyes you were born with that view things happening in real time in front of them.

Viewing physical circumstances through your physical eyes can dim the Third Eye because you might be absorbing negative imagery in others behaviors around you. The hyper focus on what's happening around you in the physical world closes the third eye chakra. This includes obsessing over media and gossip stories. Everyone was born with a Third Eye, so even if it closes, you still have access to it as you do with all of the chakras and clair channel points.

When you fear the future or hold negatively to the past and what was done to you, then this dims the third eye chakra. Looking forward fearlessly to the future and the present, while forgiving your past will assist in opening the third eye chakra. Those with a clean third eye chakra tend to be creative beings open to all that is unseen. They paint pictures with their mind and translate it into their art. They are open spiritually and to God, Heaven, and all the spirit worlds that exist.

Archangel Raziel is the one to call on to assist in cleansing and awakening your Third Eye Chakra. He stimulates spiritual sight and assists in manifesting your visions.

Crown Chakra – Violet

The Crown Chakra is the final and eighth chakra. It resides in your crown and slightly above the top of your head, which is also part of your aura. Your aura expands as great as six feet around your human body, which is why when someone sensitive is standing close to a toxic person, they are absorbing that person's energy from their aura. The aura changes color based on your mood and thoughts much like your Chakras. The crown chakra spins faster than any of the other chakras and illuminates a deep violet color.

The crown chakra is also connected to the third eye chakra. The Third Eye is what assists you in visualizing what you desire. The place of imagination begins in the crown chakra and in the mind with your thoughts. Those with strong Claircognizance tend to have a cleaner crown chakra. These are the ones who operate primarily from the analytical mind. They have the gift of clear knowing. This is where the answers to problems seem to fall right through their crown out of nowhere.

Heaven communicates through all of your channels including the crown chakra. Channelers also have a high degree of Claircognizance, as they are able to access Divine input as it drops naturally through their conscious. They are then able to translate it onto the page. As messages and input travel and drop through your crown chakra, this is communicated to other Chakras throughout your body.

Claircognizance is one of my dominating Clairs next to Clairaudience. Born with the gift of knowing has enabled me to help a great many people over the course of my life. Since early childhood I have been offering others Divine wisdom regarding issues they needed help with.

Your crown chakra is associated with your overall consciousness where Divine information flows through you. When someone lacks of consciousness, such as a terrorist, someone who bullies, name calls, antagonizes others, and feels nothing, then these are people with a dirty crown chakra. They have closed up the access to the Divine.

Words and thoughts flow through the crown chakra, so practice keeping the vibration energy of those words to ones that are positive. Activate your crown chakra by diving into reading, writing, higher learning, and research endeavors. How you perceive everything, including the world around you and what is unseen, filters through the crown chakra.

Archangel Uriel is the one to call on to help in awakening the crown chakra as he rules those with Claircognizance. He guides others with his lantern filled with light down the higher path by dropping helpful insight, ideas, and wisdom into your crown chakra.

Cleansing the Chakras

You can cleanse the chakras by getting into a calm meditative space. Visualize each of the wheels spinning counter clockwise. Then imagine God's white light shining through each of the wheels blasting away all of the dark debris latched onto these wheels. These spinning wheels are much like mini-fans. You've likely seen a fan spinning. When a fan has been used for quite some time it begins to collect dust on it. This is what it's like with your chakras. Maintenance is needed to keep your chakras clear from debris. You can do that with the power of visualization, or by changing your behavior and thought patterns associated with that particular chakra.

When you plague your mind of thoughts of fear or lack of money, then your Root Chakra becomes dirty. When you repress your sexuality and creativity, you clog the Sacral Chakra. When you give your power away to others, you dirty up your Solar Plexus Chakra. When you live victimized over what a past lover did to you, then you block the Heart Chakra. If you keep your thoughts to yourself and do not speak your truth, then you dirty up your Throat Chakra. If you absorb negative words and sounds around you, then your Ear Chakra becomes dusty. If you don't believe in the imagination or spiritual truth, then you block the Third Eye Chakra. And when you lack of consciousness and think negative thoughts, you muddy up your Crown Chakra. All chakras have white sparkly diamond like lights in them when they are fully functioning. The opposite of that are black and brown spots in various sizes within it.

*C*hapter Thirteen

Channeling Creatively

*M*y Spirit team's perspective is different than the outlook of the people living an Earthly life, including myself at times. They give me another angle to peer through in a sense. The way I view things is split in parts. One of those parts is that I have a human ego and get affected over certain day to day practical things to a degree as any other person. I'm able to take it more in stride and have it roll off with the assistance and connection with my Spirit team. Others around me have used the phrase, "Calm inside the storm." While everyone is running around creating or swirling around in drama, I'm unaffected with unmoving rock like strength. In my earlier years, I wasn't working with my team daily the way I began to as I grew older. The days I didn't work with them were highly noticeable. For instance, issues that popped up were more dramatic, heightened, intense, and all over the place. With Heaven's intervention, the issues were less intense and resolved quicker. I grew to learn they were trying to get my attention in order to work with them like any team. I realized that I didn't need to go it completely alone.

One other part of me is the consciousness of my Spirit team. This part of me has an emotionally detached aerial view of circumstances once the dark side of my ego and blocks are dissolved or reduced. Sometimes the answers Spirit gives me are not necessarily what one wants to hear. Nor are they answers that would give one peace of mind depending on how your ego takes it. There is a separation between who I am and the spirit guidance offered.

Falling into a channel for me can happen naturally, effortlessly, and within seconds. It takes longer if I've absorbed in someone else's drama, which I do my best to avoid. No matter how hard you try to dodge it, sometimes it lands on your lap for whatever reason, or you accidentally walk right into it carelessly.

The transition from the human part of me to my team happens within seconds. I might walk away giggling at some obscene practical joke I've played on someone and walk into the next room. I sit down, and move both my hands over my crown and over my face mentally calling in my team and now I'm in the channel. My Spirit team has the steering wheel and I'm in the passenger seat kicking back. There is an evident distinction between their helpful compassion to my personal crass extremism.

Heaven understands you're going through human experiences they cannot relate to since it is not the world they live in. They reside in a place that is all love, all knowing, uplifting joy, happiness, serenity, and peace. There is no antagonism, bullying, domination, and unkindness where they are.

They view Earthly life behind a glass studying human behavior and actions like a therapist. They know the basis for life and the reasons things happen. They know the truth and reality that blindsides the ego. Even if the spirit in Heaven had once lived an Earthly life, they did during a time in Earth's history that is radically different than it is now. History and humanity is ever evolving at a slow pace, but it is evolving. It would progress much quicker if the human ego were more accepting of other people. To not do so is naïve, animalistic, and primal.

You're having a human experience and with that there will be hurt, pain, and suffering. There are times where you invited it in unpretentiously, and other times where it was beyond your control. Your best friend was murdered as you both innocently left a restaurant. Neither invited it in because there are people who grew up to be bad by running their life from the darkness of their ego.

The messages from Heaven come in clear and effortlessly when you are calm, peaceful, centered, and in an environment that matches those traits. Heavenly bliss is the state to thrive for and attain in order to access spirit information and guidance. Nature is an especially vital atmosphere for a writer or any creative artist to create in. Creative artists have a higher frequency of sensitivity that allows them to receive input from the other side, even if they're unaware this is where it's coming from. Messages and guidance filter in through your *etheric* senses, which are undetected by the physical part of you. It often sifts into you in a way that is not always clear. The information you receive can be discombobulated and all over the place depending on what state you are in.

My state of mind moves into a space where my consciousness is taken over by my Spirit team. When that happens, I have sudden volcanic energy bursts of messages flying in that I have to write out quickly before the moment is gone. The energy is fast paced and high that makes me feel like I can run a marathon. There is a small window before the door is shut again. Physical demands and life circumstances can play a part in that. I grow agitated if interrupted while in that high. This disruption is like being abruptly shaken awake from sleep in a frenzied force.

Once that natural high euphoria has reached its peak, my energy level suddenly and dramatically falls to the ground without warning, and so do the words. The door to Heaven has slammed quickly shut and I'm no longer in the channel zone. I'm slumped over or on the floor trying to regain life force and energy to stand up. It can take a little while before I reach that state again, but I can get there quicker when I'm in a serene nature setting. Nature surroundings are a stronger environment to take a walk in afterwards. This is not as effective when you live in a noisy area that has too many people and cars. What also helps is going for a walk, jogging, hiking, or biking. Movement and physical activity is good to do no matter how much energy has been drained from the channeling session.

Mediums communicate with those who crossed over to the other side and relay messages to those on the Earth plane wanting to converse with their deceased loved one who are residing in another plane. Mediums are channeling, but channeling has a slightly differing goal than Mediumship. Channelers will communicate information from more than one being or entity such as a team of Guides, whereas a Medium is connecting with a departed loved one on the other side.

As a channeler, I communicate with a higher-level team of Spirit Guides, Guardian Angels, Saints, and Archangels primarily for the purpose of my work. My work is done through the written word in books. The words are intended to empower, inspire, and teach others who are interested or ready for the information. Sometimes one is guided to a book of mine by their Spirit team because there might be one sentence you needed to read that is the answer to a question that has been up in the air for some time. I cannot articulate the messages efficiently through speaking. My mind moves too fast to verbalize it at times. It's easier for me to sit down and write it all out without distraction. It also comes out clearer pending my state of mind is free of toxins. Have you ever tried to email someone when you're upset? The email dictated comes out all wrong and nonsensical. You re-read it later and say, "Why did I send this?"

Describing how Channeling works is like a gifted actor attempting to describe their process. Popular working actors have said they read the text on the page and interpret the words as best they can. Every actor has a different method and there is no right or wrong way. It is whatever works successfully for that person. This is the same way that your psychic intuitive gifts might be stronger with Clairsentience, but weaker with Claircognizance. Everyone's gifts vary from one person to the next. Channeling works in this same fashion where other channelers communicate in a variety of different ways that are not similar to the way someone else does it.

I've been channeling naturally since I was born, even though I never attributed a word to what I was doing. It's not like they teach this stuff in school, although they should. People would be more connected and in tune, which would result in their life experiences being smoother and less troublesome. Those who want to thrive in the world of business, political, or legal arenas would be even more successful if they were in tune.

As a child, I could hear voices of spirit communicating to me. Sometimes they spoke individually and other times in unison. I knew they weren't on this plane, but it felt like they were in the next room or standing next to me. I'd be outside playing and I could hear them talking to me. At the time as a child, I described it as people located somewhere else. They have always been like a loving, yet teaching counsel of souls, and yet they seemed to be right there with me travelling along wherever I went. I never thought of it as strange or different. They were never cruel and have always been kind and loving. I thought of them as my best friends outside of the physical human friendships. This is because they listened to me and heard my problems and offered assistance that helped me in some way. They knew and know everything about me, every secret, and every tiny shred of hidden nuances. They would tell me things that were about to happen and then it would come to light. It is the one area I have always felt truly loved unconditionally. They have my back no matter what.

When it's all you know, then you don't think twice about it. I assumed that everyone was doing it, but I gradually discovered most were not paying much attention to it. I later learned from my team that they could if they tuned in. My team had me go through exercises that showed me what would block it and what would open up that connection.

Some religious followers use their words to harm others or put them down and say that it is coming from God. Those who are non-believers will then retaliate and say that anyone who says their words are coming from God is a crazy person. Both of these extreme points are false. God is everywhere. He is in every cell, atom, and ion that exists. He is the energy that makes up every centimeter on the planet, and the universe, and all dimensions. He is within every human soul, animal, plant, you, and even the most harmful hate filled person. There is no escape from Him. The best parts of you are what God is, and the worst parts are your ego, also known as the Devil. The only destruction and corruption going on in the world is done at the hands of humankind.

It doesn't matter what someone believes or does not believe, because He grants all living energy free will choice even if it's not true. The purpose for that is to help your soul learn, grow, and evolve. You don't learn, grow, and evolve unless you're granted the freedom to choose and experience things for yourself. You can stay stuck in a negative mindset or despise other people, but the only person it hurts in the end is you. It stunts your soul's growth even if you cannot see that it has at that moment. There is no clarity when the ego is running the show. At the end of your life run, the truth becomes clear as you are shown images of all your human years on the planet and what you did or did not do with it. You're shown what you said or did not say to someone. This includes how that affected you and the other person, whether it was a loved one, or an acquaintance, or stranger. You experience those emotions through all perceptions.

Everyone is connected to God because there is no way you cannot be. It is easy to determine who is picking up on the voices of God and who is not. God has the highest vibration traits possible and imaginable. This means when you exude high vibration traits such as love, joy, and peace, then you are connected to God. When you exude traits that are the opposite of that such as hate, pain, negative feelings, and emotions, then you are disconnected from God. What this also means is that someone can be a practicing religious person who goes to Church regularly, or works in a Church, and yet they are unaware they are disconnected from God.

You do not need to go into a Church to communicate with God. The media portrays cruel intentions born out of a religious person so it gives all religious followers a bad name, but there are both good and bad people in every group that exists on the planet. You don't hear about the good, because the media consistently feeds you the darkness. Therefore, one comes to the conclusion that it must be all people in that group that are bad since that is all you hear.

An atheist or non-believer can be displaying compassionate, loving, and giving traits to others and IS connected to God more than they would believe. It doesn't matter if you go to Church every week and have crosses adorned all over your house. If the actions you display are of a low vibration or negative, then you have no connection with God in that

145

moment.

I'm overtly sensitive to the point where it has been an issue in the practical world. It is that sensitivity gauge, which has enabled me to connect and communicate with a team of guides and angels as if one were pouring a glass of water or flicking on a light switch. Those who are equally sensitive and in tune understand this since it's something they experience as well. It is not limited to certain people as every soul that exists is able to connect when they incorporate certain practices and lifestyle changes that enhance and awaken these gifts.

A practicing psychic has higher degrees of connection, because they do it regularly. When you do anything regularly, then you become better at it. You know to steer clear of drama, toxins, and negative people as much as possible. You're not going to go to the grocery store at high noon on a weekend day. You're not going to hang out on media sites or phone apps where harsh egotistical words are darted at and around you.

I was able to successfully submerge myself into the practical world and function like any other material driven human being. Deep down I found the practical world jarring and those in it to be lacking of compassion, soul, and heart. The dark side of humanity is aloof, cruel, and self-absorbed. The only way to function in that nonsense and to get through it was to drown myself in addictions and distractions such as drugs, alcohol, cigarettes, and other time wasters. I discovered that these addictions also contributed to me being unable to fully hear the voices of Spirit. My Spirit team taught me that these addictions dimmed the communication channel to them. I'm a perfectionist, but I've never protested to be perfect....mostly. Excellence is what I thrive for and I'm just as hard on myself as I am on anyone else. Like Heaven, I know that human souls are capable of going the distance and striving for excellence within and without if they have the passion and desire. To not do so is out of laziness or indifference.

When you fine tune your senses, then there is no telling what you can do. Creative people in the arts tend to be exceptional channelers. This includes musicians, singers, actors, artists, and writers. They have a strong measure of feeling able to walk in others shoes. They have a greater capacity of input in understanding all things beyond. They channel to write music, lyrics, books, and performing. This channeled information filters into them from above.

Some Mediums meditate to get into a trance like state. The reason this is an effective method is because you're taking at least a few minutes to quiet your mind. You're silencing everything around you in order to have a stronger connection with the other side. When you quiet your thoughts and the noise of the outside world, then there is room for Spirit and God to come rushing in. Silencing everything is by removing any traces of negativity from your aura. If you're upset about something, then this will make it difficult to channel until you let that go and release it.

For me, the connection comes and goes throughout the day depending on what my state of mind is like at any given moment. I'm an ever flowing neurotic emotional mess, so when I'm moved into a state of reception, then the messages and guidance flows into my soul through one of my Clair channels and the connection is made. Asking for the connection to be made while in a meditative state doesn't always work for me since I operate on an adrenaline rush. Being in the channel, the connection smashes in without warning. The frequency waves in my brain move up and down on their own while I'm doing other things until there is a connection, then I stop and sit down to recite the information flowing in. It's almost like the tides of the ocean are constantly moving, and so is the frequency channel within my soul. If I'm disconnected at any moment, that state can change three minutes later out of nowhere.

I will stare at a blank page of a potential manuscript for days and even weeks and then bam the channel connection is made. The information is either dictated to me clairaudiently *(etheric hearing sense)* or it's all dumped into my mind in one sitting through claircognizance *(etheric knowing sense)* like a tidal wave gushing over land. Sometimes they'll show me visuals through clairvoyance *(etheric seeing sense)*.

The first step to getting closer to channeling naturally is by being aware of your own soul and what's outside of it. When you pay attention and notice all of the physical distracting noises, then you're able to diminish those sounds. You can do that when you're out and about in a busy area such as a street or at a mall.

Perk up your ears hearing the noisy symphonic sounds coming from the rumbling of cars, tires skidding, the wind blowing, the birds chirping and so on. Listen to the sounds of the garbage cans banging, sirens going off, people talking, or shouting. Notice the distracting energy on your phone and the things you aim your focus towards while on it. The key is being aware when it has become a distraction. Once you're able to notice these differences, you not only realize how distracted the planet is, but you're then able to work on dissolving those sounds in your mind and tune it out. When it is tuned out, the noise level of spirit begins to rise. Spirit is already loud, but when it sounds as if they're non-existent, far away, or muted, it is because the sounds of the physical part of the world are turned up way too high. Those sounds include the noise of your own thoughts. It's like you're blasting your music at home, and you and a guest are trying to talk over it. You keep saying, "What?" Finally, you turn the music down a little and you can hear one another. Turning the physical distractions down enables one to hear the voice of Heaven clearer.

When I fall into the channel space for a project, then no interruptions are allowed. I will not look at anything, or read anything submitted to me, even if it's an email, unless it's urgent from a best friend, family member, or love interest. Breaking this rule interferes with the process and flow of input. I've made the mistake in the past to break away from the channel to look at someone's manuscript, email, or message. Or I might take the time to respond to a novella email from a new pen pal wanting to shoot the breeze. Unfortunately, I soon discover that this is a mistake. Not because I do not love and enjoy communicating with others, but because breaking away to do that also knocks me out of the channel momentum flow. It can destroy the creative process for the day or even weeks before I find that groove again. Those who are in my immediate circle already know and understand this process. They never complain or take it personally. This is why I soon adopted a strict unbreakable policy to never look at anything while in that space.

Once the connection is made during the creative process, I separate and disappear for a while. This is also similar to the process of a working actor. One of the well-known actresses I know will not communicate with anyone while she's filming a movie, except her agent, family, or business emergencies. Once the movie is over, then she's reaching out to all of us to come and play. Authentic creative souls understand this process very well.

Souls have been channeling Medium's since Earth's conception. Mediumship is one of the basic ways of communicating for a soul, yet this faded over the centuries as the darkness of human ego rose to prominence cutting off the connection with all things beyond the physical. Mediumship rose to popularity again as a fad around the 19th Century. The second you read words that say, *claim* or *purported*, when dealing with psychic phenomena or Mediumship, then that is when you should move on to another source. There are websites and wiki type pages that do not properly or efficiently relay information they have no business conveying. It's not a subject they are versed in enough to be discussing. You do not need a skeptic delivering you information. When you deliver information to another, keep in mind of what Heaven's set of guidelines are. They include that you only state what you're being told by them to others in a way that is objective and compassionate. Say what you see and hear, but do not instruct the person what to do. Only go as far as to say, "If you do this, then this is what will happen." If the other person says, "Which one should I do?" The response should be, "That's up to you to decide." Your best friends or family might tell you what to do, but when you go to an objective party, then they should remain neutral. This includes not telling someone that their death or someone close to them is imminent.

I've been the go to person for assistance since I was a kid. This is as far back as a teenager in High School, where others would come to me for guidance and assistance. It would only blow up in bigger ways as I grew older. One of the big things others have said since then would be that they always feel like they can tell me anything and that I do not judge. They will say half way through their story, "I can't believe I'm telling you this. I've never said this to anyone before, not even my wife." If I'm personally anti-adultery and someone is talking to me about how they cheated in a love relationship, I come from a place of non-judgment. They can tell me their deepest darkest and most offensive secrets and I have zero criticisms, which is the space that the angels come from in the channel. I separate my personal ego beliefs while I'm in the higher regions of spirit communication.

Telekinesis is a form of mind manipulation where one is able to make things happen with the power of the mind. This doesn't mean that someone can take down a building if they think it. With enough mind power, it is possible they can manipulate something to happen that is on the same energetic wavelength.

Telekinesis has been used on the weather. These weather modifications are more often than not minor shifts. The weather forecast is typically projected about ten days out. If I know I'm going to need to be doing something on a specific day and I need the weather to be tolerable, then I will pay attention to when the projected forecast is available to me. I'm a bit of a baby and cannot function when the weather is below seventy degrees. I enjoy warmer climates. Luckily, I live in Southern California where the weather is pretty consistent most of the year. If ten days out I see the projected forecast is set at 65 degrees, then I will scoff displeased. It's supposed to be a beach day or an outdoor outing and I need it warm. I move into a centered space and communicate with my Guides and Angels to raise the temperature on that particular day. I'm flexible and offer anything in the 70's or 80's, but I'll accept 70's. Days later I will check the projected weather forecast and I've noticed that the 65-degree forecast has now risen astronomically to 80 degrees. I'll smile pleased and say, "Thank you."

Extreme changes in the weather will be near impossible. If it is 20 degrees in an area where snowy winter is common, you're more than likely not going to be able to suddenly make it 80 degrees. The temperature fluctuations are minor, but in my case were significant enough to notice. This might sound absurd, but it is an example that has happened in reality here and there over time.

Most people do not request or think about things like this so there is little to no challenges in the way of manipulating it. Human souls live in a world of detachment to anything beyond the Internet and physical distractions. They drive from place to place, work on computers, have negative thoughts, and emotions, or they work a job until they drop. They're not thinking of bigger things outside of themselves, let alone altering the weather. Most either do not believe in telekinesis being possible or have never heard of it, although it was common during the historical days when there were very little physical distractions.

Weather altering is not unusual, but today others might sneer at it due to their attachment to the materialistic physical world that dominates human life. The Native American Indians altered the weather back in the day sometimes through chanting and dance. They were and are some of the great Sages in Earth's history having incarnated from the realm of the Wise Ones. Others have joked about the rain dance that Indians have done as if it is an old wives tale. The European settlers who pushed the Indians out scoffed at the spiritual ways of the Native Americans. They believed it to be hocus pocus, witchcraft, and superstition. These same bullying settlers who took over the land forced others to conform to their fictionalized religion. This is still going on today on other levels.

As a result, they sentenced Indians to jail time for decades when they refused to convert. These same settlers hung or burned those they believed to be witches. Those who showcased a greater range of spiritual gifts, or seemed more in tune to things outside of the mundane were considered to be dangerous and born out of the spawn of Satan. They did everything in their power to get rid of them so that they could rule. This is all power, greed, and ego. The rigid, puritanical, settlers were blocked from receiving true divine guidance from God. Their ancestors still uphold this true detachment from Spirit. Ironically the world is witnessing this with terrorists believing that if you do not convert to their beliefs, then you must die horrifically.

Everyone is born psychic whether you believe you are or not. These abilities never go away even if it feels that way. They are hanging out under the surface and always accessible. When you don't feel psychic, it just means something is blocking it. Blocks can be certain toxic foods, drinks, negative moods, bad energy, technological distractions, and other people to name a few. The closer you are to the physical Earth and nature, the easier your abilities can begin the process of being re-awakened. The physical Earth is anything that is not manmade, such as buildings and cars. Certain lifestyle changes need to be incorporated into your life as well such as stripping yourself of potential blocks.

What a spectacular gift it is to have the luxury of life everlasting. Your life is intended to be about love. Your soul in your body craves this love full time. Say goodbye to the dead part of you, and all that no longer serves your higher good, and welcome in a brand new Phoenix rising gradually emerging and bursting out at the seams dying to get out and soar. You are alive, awakened, ignited, and ready for the most incredible ride up ahead. Make everyday count and spread love like you never have before.

Love is beyond love and relationships. It's treating people with love and respect unless of course they're cruel to you. Correct them using assertiveness or walk away from the dark energy. I've been studying the human condition since I was a teen, but it was also something implanted into my soul since I incarnated here. I've been around the block quite a bit by having street smart experiences that others typically avoid or shy away from. I infuse my Spirit team's guidance and messages that help others along with the street smarts class I received this lifetime and all lifetimes before it. I'm a teacher of love and respect. It's one of the top things I care about before anything else.

One of the common questions I receive is, "How do I connect in a channel with Heaven?" I'm unable to efficiently explain it since it wasn't something I was trained to do. The channel connection has been happening since I was a kid. As early as seven years old this team of voices that were not in front of me was talking to me, and I was listening. These weren't the crazy voices or the ego voice, since neither of those voices predicts or lays out things to come that end up happening. Nor do they instruct one to harm themselves or someone else. I didn't meditate. I didn't use props. It just happened whenever it wanted to. It's always been like that even though I can choose to light a candle and put on soft music to get me into a more relaxed state.

If I need to work (write) and I'm not in the zone, then it's not happening. The zone is what I call the higher frequency vibrations that are raised to reach my teams vibrations, which are lowered. This way there is a match and you're both in this zone. If I'm all over the place and undisciplined, then it's not happening. But it's also like calling a friend who isn't home. They're aware I need to connect. I keep calling and calling periodically throughout the day, then bam suddenly the connection is made out of nowhere and everything is flying in at once. I'm relieved to be in that space because it's a total rush and high, better than any drug or drink.

A Connecting Exercise:

Find a comfortable spot to sit and relax. Breathe in deeply and exhale, then repeat breathing in and then out as you grow more relaxed. On every exhale, breathe out all traces of negativity. Breathe out any pain, hurt, or sadness you're holding inside. Breathe out all of that toxic emotion. Breathe out elements of residual anger and any level or form of upset. Breathe out any envy, jealousy, doubts, and all hints of negative toxins and emotions.

Whenever you *breathe in* imagine you are breathing in the light. Drink in this light whenever you inhale. Allow the light to envelope you inside and out. Imagine it is diminishing and dissolving all lower energies. Allow it to blast away all remaining negativity in you. Breathe in and drink in this light. Exhale this light so that it is blown out and filling up your aura around your soul and body. Now you are bathing in this light inside and out. Every time you breathe, the light grows bigger and begins to sparkle. There is no escape from this light as it fills you up lifting you into a peaceful serene love and joyful feeling. Visualize and feel yourself being surrounded by this light of God lifting your vibration up.

Chapter Fourteen

Unleashing the Creative Spirit

Introverted and shy human souls have a higher quotient of creativity flowing through their spirit. Introversion and shyness are two separate traits. Someone can be an introvert, but not shy at all, whereas an extrovert can be shy. Someone who is shy might be misconstrued to be an introvert when that's not always the case. Introverts keep to themselves or prefer higher bouts of alone time than an extrovert. It can be difficult for them to connect with others even if they crave human stimulation once in awhile. There are many ways that an introverted creative soul can connect with other likeminded people. While technology has its cons, there are the obvious benefits to devices such as social media or phone apps. You can take your time getting to know others on a phone app or a social media page before you are comfortable enough to take it to the next level. The next steps preceding that are personal email, text, and then phone conversations. If you cannot have a phone conversation, then how are you going to be making it through an in person *hang out?* The next step is followed by meeting in person. My own professional social media page has surprisingly brought some of my readers/followers together in long term friendships. This is by recognizing one another's positive statements to my posts. They start to learn about one another while hanging out in my house that is my social media page. Soon they interact with one another and eventually take it off my page and onto their own pages.

Other ways of connecting with those like you is to take a class. This can be online or a physical class room, both of which you can interact with other students. Taking a class in the area or genre of your interest assists in awakening the creative part of you and opens the door to getting to know others who have similar interests.

When you communicate via social media or a phone app, be sure to put in an effort with others by opening up beyond a few words. I've discovered through hands on research others barely put in more than a one to five-word sound bite that is similar to the person before them. If you're a highly creative soul, then this shouldn't be too much of an issue since you can find creative ways to string words together to catch the other person's attention. The most nerve wracking challenge will be when you and this other person meet face to face, but by that time you'll likely be so familiar with each other that it won't be that difficult.

Some of the other positive benefits to following social media pages or taking classes in the area of your interest are that higher learning and interacting with other likeminded souls stimulates inspiration. It pulls you out of a lull you might be experiencing and activates your mind, and raises your energy levels, and focus.

Inspiration is a key component to achieve when looking to get creative. Find ways to bring on inspiration such as taking regular time outs to walk through a nature setting. Take long weekend getaways to a serene place of your choice that can inspire you. Any place bathed in nature can help with inspiration from the beach, mountains, desert, lakes, or any open nature preserve with little to no people. Go to a museum, art gallery, listen to motivating music, read a book, or watch a movie. Those are some of the things I do to get inspired. I also find inspiration in other people. My love relationships or romantic dates have helped me by acting as a muse.

The soul starves for stimulation and creativity. Express yourself artistically without censure or fear that others will not approve or like what you do. You don't have to share your art with the world if you choose not to. It can be for your eyes only, or something you share with a loved one, or your close trusted circle around you. This is assuming that those who are immediately close to you are people you can trust and express yourself freely with. I've discovered from being approached by readers that they feel they can be more open with me, a stranger, than someone in their immediate circle. While this is a nice compliment, the reverse should be true. One should have at least one person in their life they can completely trust until the end of their days. Work on getting to know other people through social media pages, classes, destinations, and apps that promote positive common interests between you.

Unleashing the creative spirit in you contributes to success in your life on all levels. Creative people seek out ways to stimulate that part of their soul for the sake of release. When done positively, they engage in activities that are stimulating to their mind. A successful soul reads, researches, and partakes in positive activities, while an unsuccessful soul is sedentary, surfs the Internet, or sits around drinking bottles of alcohol, watching television all day, or chatting with others on apps out of boredom.

I've been doing extensive research into the human condition my entire life. We watched the rise of technology bring down the masses. There are positive benefits of course, but no one reads, no one educates themselves, or takes the time to walk in someone else's shoes. If you believe in something they don't, then they take it upon themselves to send you a toxic negative diatribe against you. They follow and adopt whatever the media or their peers feed them and believe it to be Gospel. There are few who can carry deep compassionate meaningful conversations even if you disagree with someone. The current reality is that it is near non-existent. Arguing and antagonism is at the forefront instead.

There is no exploration, intelligence, or branching away from the crowd to investigate, research, and discover the deeper answers because no one cares. Attention spans are stunted and posting sound bites is in. Conversations fizzle out as quickly as they start up. This has carried over to the demise of long term love relationships to be short lived. Some make excuses such as open relationships are in and monogamy is out. They believe we're not designed to last with the same person until the end of our lives. Even though for centuries we had no problem doing that without complaint. We also have no struggle with it back home in Heaven, since little ego is used. It was only once technology, popular culture, and rebelliousness took off did that effect shut down long-term relationships. People today have a hard time working together in a union for life. There is too much ego to include another person's feelings and desires.

These are all arguments to justify egotistical selfish behavior and mask the fact that the reasons long term relationships don't last is because people have short attention spans and grow bored with what they have after five minutes. No one cares about anybody or anything anymore. They pretend to when someone famous dies for a couple of days, but then they're obsessing over the next big media story. They're governed by their ego and what they desire at that moment. If it's no longer on par with the one they're with, then they leave them instead of compromising and finding a middle ground. They end up with someone new that lasts for a short time and that ends the same way. It's a repetitive cycle that ceases to end. Those who are single want to be in a relationship and those in a relationship fantasize about being single. You want the opposite of what you have at any given moment. All of this is brought up because it strangles the creative spirit right out of you.

Healthy creative souls are the ones who are more likely to compliment others on their positive traits, while unhealthy souls will criticize you, and post negative words in comments or online. The unhealthy unsuccessful soul sits around gossiping about people, while the successful soul is animated and excitedly discusses things they want to do and accomplish.

Diving into a creative project or functioning from the artistic side of you helps in removing blocks. These blocks prevent good stuff from flowing to you. It cuts off the communication connection line with your own spirit, and your team in Heaven.

If you're a creative soul who enjoys the creative process, but also sells your art to consumers, then you understand the dynamic beyond being creative in the privacy of your own home. Having a career in the creative arts makes you susceptible to criticism from the public. The irony is the creative person is also a sensitive on a deeper level, so it's important to do your best in separating the reality of what you do from harsh critics. All that matters is that you partake in work that is meaningful to YOU. When you put that expression out into the world, then release the desire to absorb any criticism that happens to come your way. As for any measure of success you crave from your work, side business, or hobby, keep the faith that it will happen.

Remain optimistic while you continue working at your hobby and art. If it's something you enjoy doing no matter what, then it won't feel like work to you. You'll do it regardless if there is any monetary gain in it. Many success stories from popular artists admit that the success came to them out of nowhere. Suddenly they began to see a gradual rise or immediate shot of financial success fly into their life. When you love and enjoy what you're doing, then you're infusing this love enjoyment energy into your work. This is a positive ingredient that will attract a likeminded energy to it. If you do your work with fear and worry, then you will likely attract that kind of negative crowd base to it. The energy will be a block that prevents success from entering the picture. Stay positive, optimistic, and joyful with all that you do when you can help it.

I receive my fair share of criticism, although it is minimal in comparison to those who appreciate some of my books. I've been receiving harsh criticism from others since I was a kid. By the time I became an author, I was already indifferent and detached from those who take issue with what I do, or how I do it, or who I am. I don't care if someone doesn't like me or not. Nor do I care if they like what I do. They don't have a say in it. I'm not doing my work for them and I'm not going to stop because of them. I own my life and I live it for me as should you. If I don't care about something or someone, I don't give it any energy or attention. It's not interesting enough for me to bother.

I've worked with well-known talent during my tenure in the Entertainment business. These celebrities know to stay away from reading gossip about themselves or read comments under articles about them. I've never heard of any cases where they fold and read any of that stuff. Most of them are too productive and busy to notice. When you're busy with life you don't have time for boredom that leads to reading articles about oneself. Not only are the comments and articles not based in reality, but it's not healthy or beneficial for you on any level to soak in that energy.

I've witnessed what it's like from the perspective of a famous artist. To me, they're no different than any other friend or colleague, but then you realize they are super popular and many in the world love and admire their work. There are just as many people in the world who despise or criticize them unfairly and negatively. They say things about them that are not true, but you ignore that and stay focused on what's important. It's like someone saying negative toxic things on the news about someone you're close to. You don't know why or where that's coming from. It appears bizarre and peculiar that a stranger is talking about someone they know nothing about personally.

Avoid allowing anyone to stop you from doing what you love. Ignore the naysayers and stay strong in faith knowing that you are loved no matter what you do or who you are. There will always be a critic out there who has something to say.

Focus on your work and creating, then put it out into the world if that's what you choose to do. If you do that, then when you release it into the world, you're also releasing the need to concern yourself over anyone who happens to like it or not. You create your art for yourself, and then you share it with those in the world who are interested and positively benefit from it. There will always be someone who doesn't like you, or what you do, so you have to get over that. It's not your issue to wrestle with.

Steer clear of all drama and negativity in others around you. This includes strangers who criticize you – not to mention those who are allegedly intended to be close to you. There is a difference between helpful constructive criticisms from those around you as opposed to plain old nasty criticism from strangers. The difference is that constructive criticism is someone who is close to you who've you asked their opinion on something and they've given you a critique.

It's like an editor of a writing piece who suggests to the writer, "*You might want to consider opening the book with this paragraph instead of that one as it'll immediately pull the reader in with shock.*"

Constructive criticism comes from a place of love where the person wants you to succeed. The opposite side of this kind of criticism is someone who is jealous of who you are and what you can do. They attack instead of offering helpful comments that benefit.

There are some people who are afraid to dive into anything artistic related for fear of criticism. The ego part of them convinces one that it will be of no use. The more you do something, the easier it gets and the better you are at it. This can be anything in life from a job you take that you've never done before, to any creative interests you dive into. You dread being exposed and vulnerable as if you're in some form of danger due to your high sensitivity. This anxiety is part of your ego mind and not based in truth. Avoid altering your creative work to appeal to the masses or out of panic that someone won't like it. When you do that you are distancing yourself from authenticity. This is seen with popular music acts that conform to the current market to remain significant to popular culture at that time, instead of creating authentically the way they did when they first started their career. They were once a trendsetter in the process because of this realism.

Your creative spirit is intended to be solely you and who you are buried deep within, and not what someone else wants or will want to see. If they want to see something, then let them create their own thing. This isn't about creating art that you intend to sell, but this is anything you set out to do whether it's a job, a friendship, or relationship. Be your most authentic self since you can only fake it for so long before being found out.

I've done work that I've kept on a shelf for longer than it should have due to my insane unrealistic need for perfectionism. It's a level that no one can get to. If I waited until that thoroughness was there, then I would never get any work done. My Spirit team taught me in the beginning of my days to release the need to be perfect. The only thing that matters is the content and what one chooses to say. While it should be somewhat readable avoid getting lost over the fact that a comma is in the wrong place. Make it as good as you can and then move onto something else. If you get into your head wondering what if no one likes it, then just quit, lie down, and wait to die. It's a waste of time putting something off because you're not ready or it will never be perfect. What is considered perfect is based on human ego rules, which have no validity in the end anyway. You have your own individual stamp on what you choose to say or create.

In the past, I've included others in my voting processes to discover what they liked or did not like. I thought it would be fun to get everyone involved. While it was to an extent, I discovered some would get upset when you chose to go with something that did not have their seal of approval. I started to concern myself with trying to find a way to please and satisfy everybody. This ended up being useless and ineffective. It also watered down who I am and what I set out to do. I was no longer being my most authentic creative self. It is impossible to please every single person. It will never happen no matter what you do, so throw that idea out the window and just do what feels right to you in the end.

Your sensitivity is a gift that can be immersed into your creative work. Other sensitives will pick up on if you're going against who you are to please the crowd as opposed to being your true self. They will be attracted to you and your work when you do not compromise your integrity. Not only will they be fascinated, but they will relate and enjoy you even more for this authenticity.

When I obtained my first job at the record store at seventeen years old, I was initially nervous, yet excited, not knowing if I could do it. Soon I was mastering it as I mastered all jobs over the course of my life. When I got into the film business at age twenty-three, I feared I would be fired in the beginning of every film gig. The opposite ended up happening where I became a huge sought after commodity behind the scenes for studios, production companies, and talent. This is because I was soon doing the job with extreme precision and confidence. Word was spreading fast in this circus of similar creative intelligent misfits. The same nature is applied to all areas of extracurricular work I've done. I wanted to try my hands at those jobs for the experience and knowledge it entailed ranging from real estate, to legal/law, and to digital marketing. All of my past jobs were classes that I received financial compensation for. When I started each gig I didn't know anything about the genre. I was hired based on my enthusiasm and creative nature. When I chose to dissolve the employment in those arenas I did it at a point where I was on top of my game and had fully mastered the genre. All of those classes infused creative knowledge that I could impart into my work as a self-employed author. Everything you experience helps you gain confidence, knowledge, and life lessons. These traits were applied to my past love relationships, although this was not the case with my exes, which is why they are now my exes.

You deserve all measures of success whether that is inner or outer achievement. You are a soul child born with an innate knowing how to create. When you're home in Heaven on the other side, you paint the pictures of what you desire with intention. It is almost like magic due to how effortless it is. If you want to visit someone or go somewhere, you think it and you are there. The soul is limitless on the other side, and the soul is imperfect in the physical human body. You can't think *I want to be in Bali right now*, and then get transported physically there. The process is similar where you can think about being in Bali and eventually one day you will get there. Your thoughts produce circumstances. When you think or dream positive things, then that energy is catapulted outwardly and returned back to you tenfold. This is why you want to make sure you stay as positive as you can. Release any negative self-talking words from your mind and aura and know that you deserve good just as much as anyone who has experienced popular success.

Allow the vibrating power of spirit to flow through and awaken the creative part of you. Take care of yourself on all levels inside and out. This will assist in giving you greater energy, stamina, and focus, not to mention a stronger connection with your Spirit team. Having a crystal clear communication line with God will enable you to make sounder decisions in your life. It will assist you in reaching a higher vibration state than if you didn't have that connection. Creativity helps in raising your vibration into high feelings of joy, love, and peace, while boosting your faith and optimism. Diving into creative projects or obtaining a creative slant in your nature and day to day dealings also help in lifting blocks in your way to abundance.

Pay attention to the guidance your Spirit team filters in through you. When you receive a sign or message that is continuous, then this is a clue that it could be Heavenly support coming into you. The message has a positive uplifting feeling to it and will not be bathed in fear or anxiety. Sometimes one can mistake a message for being heavenly support as opposed to their ego. If you're someone who is constantly fleeing where you live or who you're romantically involved with, then this is not heavenly support, but the ego. Heavenly support has a high vibration positive feeling to it that benefits you and everyone around.

Expressing restlessness or any uncomfortable feeling through creativity is a fantastic way to release negativity from your soul. You can paint, draw, take photos, write, play music, games, make your own mix CD's, re-organize your home, put puzzles together, make fun videos, sing, dance, or anything creative at all. All creative movements get the positive energy within and around you moving again.

Many of the themes discussed in this book lead to an awakening of the creative spirit in you. This is more than working on art projects or becoming an entrepreneur and opening up your own business. Those traits are part of it, but it is also unleashing that part of you that is connected to God. The creative part of you within that is in tune to all nuances in and around you. It is your inner child that is full of love, joy, and peace around the clock. This is why detoxing and watching what you ingest were discussed. It is because these all play a factor into what drains your life force energy zapping any ounce of creativity in you. Take care of all parts of you. Watch what you ingest and the energy of the thoughts you put into your mind. Self-care is a not only a luxury, but a necessity. Love all that you are, and remember to pat yourself on the back for any job well done. When you've accomplished anything at all, then treat yourself to something good in celebration. Whether that's a hiking sabbatical trip or that t-shirt or music album you always wanted. Go for it! Reward yourself. You deserve the endless reservoirs of success and prosperity in all areas of your life that exist. Never stop being creative and live your life from the heart. Create out of love and give out of love.

Chapter Fifteen

The Creative Spirit Power
Works for Me

Born a high octane creative soul can lead you down a path of toxic addictions if you don't channel your creativity through positive outlets. All souls have access to the Divine spirit and therefore access to the creative spark within them. Some have a stronger connection to God than others, which results in a greater ability to receive psychic intuitive input. If you are a sensitive on any level, then this is a sign that you are truly gifted.

It is a challenge being an empathic sensitive soul at times. When this part of you is left to dangle without control, then it can feel as if you've been catapulted off a cliff without a parachute. You flounder all over the place feeling directionless accompanied by emotions that shoot up and down from one hour to the next. I know what this is like as this is a part of me I've wrestled with my entire life. It has led me to drug and alcohol addictions in my late teens through my early twenties. I would do and take everything possible to numb the emotional pain that consumed and suffocated me as a child.

There are the great artists the world has witnessed over the course of history as well as artists that others have not heard of universally. This is from the reclusive soul living in the middle of nowhere drawing sketches in her garden, to the young child finger painting his clairvoyant visions on a blank canvas. The creative spirit within you is the colorful ways that you express yourself. It can be the words you string together in practice before you work up the nerve to approach that guy or girl you've had crushing eyes on for so long. It's the way you organize your dresser drawers at home, to the way you perform your duties at your job. Being creative helps you think outside of the box and find solutions to problems that others have a tough time putting together. Your personality is infused with your own creative originality and imprint.

Growing up it was noticed there were two distinct sides to me, the masculine and the feminine. The masculine being the outwardly expressing little dude who would need to slow down from too much sporty physical activity, and the feminine side where my inner world was unleashed into expressive creative projects. All souls are born with an equal amount of masculine and feminine traits. Expressing them equally adds to having balance in your life.

When I was eight years old, I had an attraction to architecture and buildings. I would spend my spare time constructing fortresses and homes through hand drawn designs or cardboard pieces. One year I spent weeks putting together a castle I had recurring visions of in my mind's eye. It was a castle that I clairvoyantly saw to be my home back in Heaven. It would be decades later when I pieced that together and described as being evident in one of the worlds on the other side in my book *Realm of the Wise One*.

This castle I put together back when I was a kid was one that I wanted to move into. I spent days working on it with heavy construction paper and other tools and crafts I could get my hands onto. I created a moat, a bridge, and rooms located through a labyrinth of halls. That was the moment where I noticed those close to me visibly dropping their jaws. They came to the conclusion that I might have a creative gift, or an interest in something artistic related. They excitedly jumped up and down with glee over that.

I've always felt alive diving into artistic endeavors and in unleashing my creative spirit. When I was moody, depressed, or angry, I'd find something creative to do that dissolved those blocks and lift me back into the higher dominions of joy and optimism. Escaping into a creative world is where I've always been happiest. The world is a tragic place thanks to the darkness of ego in humankind, but in the creative world is where all love and pure enjoyment exist.

One of my cousins and I spent a Summer together as kids getting creative from carving substances like soap into creatures born out of our imagination, to building forts that spanned the entire yard out of boxes and other materials we could find. These were elaborate and time consuming taking us several weeks of fun as we watched the dream unfold into a little reality. As the fortress grew, more people in the community started to crowd around and watch the thrill take place. When we were done, we opened the gates and allowed all of the neighborhood kids to dive on into them. This unleashed their inner child and imagination, which had not yet been tampered with by jaded adults. Even the adults were mesmerized reminding them of who they once were before the physical reality took over. I always had a way of promising others a good time by taking them into a fantasy world that reminded them of what it is like to play and experience joy.

Before the age of ten I enjoyed art and architecture, but I soon discovered that writing and storytelling was beginning to dominate my life. I would tell stories to my friends in the backyard. Put on shows where I would get up behind a fake microphone and entertain through comedic stand up stories. I would take my children's books and cross sentences out and re-write them to my liking. I started carrying notepads around to write and journal anything that came to mind. By the time I moved into teen land, I was writing stories in these notepads. I knew at that point that when I would grow older, I would be an author. At the time, all I saw was that it would happen in my thirties and beyond. I didn't question it or wonder why it was further out in the distance. I didn't know how to make it happen being a fifteen-year-old kid with no money, no computer, and no anything except a vivid imagination. This was during a time when there were no cell phones or social media, and only the super rich owned a computer. And even then the computers functionality was limited.

I needed to first figure out what kind of job I could obtain to make money and survive. This would require the creative spirit part of me to exude originality in all my undertakings. With the help and connection of my Spirit team, and my strong communication channel with Heaven, they informed me that I would enjoy finding work in the film business in the entertainment industry. They guided me in steps to discover that I could get a job in the film development serious side of the business. This is the process before a film moves into Film Production and shooting. It entails story development, writing, and all of the creative aspects associated with a script before it's given a green light to film into a movie.

This is all fine and wonderful, but how would I get a job in the entertainment industry with no experience. From where I came from, I had no networking contacts with anybody. Cell phones, apps, and the Internet were not part of the human reality at that point yet. The ego part of me sadly attempted to try and convince me that I would never do anything, accomplish anything, or amount to anything. Luckily, that voice was dimmer than my higher self's voice.

Do you know how many people want to work in the film business? I realized this might take me longer than making a phone call. My team asked me what kind of regular first job I would be happy working at while I looked for film business work on the side? I said, "That's easy. Music."

My mom was big into music. She would blast her rock and roll records in the living room when she came home from work, or on the weekends as I was growing up. She would sing everywhere and anywhere freely. I had always asked, "Why didn't you try to be a professional singer?" I couldn't understand the concept of someone loving an activity, but then not trying to make it happen. Maybe it might not happen, but how do you know if you don't at least try by putting in an effort.

I used to repeatedly thumb through all of her vinyl records and gaze at each of the album covers getting lost in the artwork. They were vastly creative and not as boring as they became in the late 1990's and beyond when Cassette Tapes and Compact Discs became the rave.

Mom would take us kids to the record stores regularly. I found those trips to be the most fun. I'd get lost in the store thumbing through all of the music staring at the covers of the albums and absorbing how fantastically creative they were. I loved music and had fantasies of being a rock star musician playing the bass, a guitar, and drums. The closest I would get to that would be obtaining my first job in a music record store when I was seventeen. This was during a time when record stores existed. Those were great days when record stores and book stores were plentiful. You could get lost in the aisles for hours escaping into these creative wonderlands.

I worked at the most popular record store in the state at the time. How I got that job with no experience was by being creative in my letters to the Store Manager. I would handwrite them since I didn't have a computer. This fascinated the Store Manager enough to want to meet and hire me. Years later when I was in the film business, the store manager and I had remained in touch. During one dinner get together, she shared with me that she still had the letters I wrote to her when I was seventeen. I insisted she throw them away. She said smiling with enthusiasm, "No, I love them! That's why I kept them."

I also had a love for film and acting because of the varying world's it created on screen. Most well-known gifted actors did not go after the acting trade to be famous. If that's one's sole purpose for trying to be an actor, then you'll be greatly disappointed. These actors discovered that expressing themselves creatively through the art of inhabiting a character helped them release years of repression. The fame and money for some of them just happened to be compounded onto having a job where they could play make believe.

While working at the record store, I would come up with creative ways to try and get into the film business. I sent my cover letter and resume to hundreds of Production Companies. This was before email took off and snail mail or phone was the way to go. I got a call from the television Producers at *Carsey-Werner* at the start of 1996. They are famous for producing shows like, "Roseanne", "The Cosby Show" and "That 70's Show". The development person at the time called me into meet with her. While there, she said what caught her eye was how creative my letter was. She pointed out that I admitted to not having any experience yet, but that I added, *"I was going to apply for the role of senior vice president, but I figured you would expect one to work their way up."* She said my letter was the only one that widened her eyes and made her smile. She added she was dying to call me in and meet the person that was exceptional and bold.

There were a few production companies I cold called and left messages on their voice mail with by telling them who I was and what I could offer them. This caught the eyes, or ears I should say, of the

Development Director at actress Michelle Pfeiffer's production company, Via Rosa. We got on a phone call and spoke for a half hour like two friends who had known each other for decades. To make a long story short, she fell in love with me and asked when we could meet. I went into the offices and we hit it off again in person. She received Michelle and her partner Kate's approval, then I was hired weeks later in April 1996. This kicked off my creative life professionally a month after my twenty-third birthday. All great things came down from that up through the present day.

I was in paradise for years working with these three creative women. One of them being a big movie star at the time, and who is nothing like the stereotype people think of when it comes to Hollywood. They were the first ones to tell me that I could write. To have some pretty big talent telling a little twenty-three-year-old with no experience that he's got something special gave me external confidence that I typically relied on giving to myself. I, along with Heaven, believe in me even if no one else will.

Years in, Michelle chose to dissolve her company, but I had already met and networked with some other big talent in the industry. This led me to work in Film Production where it was one gig after another without a break. I wanted to immerse myself in all aspects of the creative world. The Film Business was a second family to me. It is true to an extent that once you're in, you stay in, but the truth is that working hard, using your creative wits, and having persistence helps immensely. It's a separate creative world in the Entertainment Business. When you meet others in that business you become instant family members no matter what. It's like a travelling tribe of eccentric creative performers that have your back whether you're in front of the camera or behind the scenes. You have a second hand telepathic connection with one another and a friendship is automatically assumed based on that common similarity.

I attained success working in the entertainment business. This success was not only financial, as I made more than I ever had at that time, but the success was also inner spiritual victory. Some of this had to do with the innovative and creative ways I performed all of my jobs. I mastered ways of doing and running things that others around me admired and soon adopted and incorporated into the way they worked.

As I mentioned, I always knew that I would eventually become an author. Once again, I needed to have my creative wits about me and come up with ways that I could begin making that dream come true. I've spent my entire life feeling at home working on creative projects, whether this was building a castle out of construction paper, to handwriting stories in a journal, to working with Hollywood's top talent in massive creative environments, to writing books for those interested or guided to them. Even if no one was interested, I would still be doing it. It is pure joy getting to unleash my creative spirit in innovate ways professionally.

Figuring out what to do that is creative based will come at the right time. When you struggle to receive a message from your Spirit team, then this creates a resistance block. It pushes the message further away from you. This same concept is similar to receiving creative inspiration. Creativity is channeled divine inspiration, which does not necessarily come automatically. Have patience and let go of the need to receive inspiration.

If you don't feel you belong in this world, then this is a sign that you're here to contribute some measure of positive change towards humanity and the evolving planet. It doesn't have to be grand. It can be by shining and exuding that bright light in your soul onto others through love and compassion. It can be immersing your spirit into the creative arts. This is helping the world change one person at a time.

As a creative being, information will not instantly come to you. Artists have spoken about needing a muse to offer artistic insight. If a creative artist is not feeling inspired, it's difficult to create. This applies to anyone looking to get creative since you are a creative being, even if creativity is not something you partake in much. Regardless, the ability to be creative is present in you. Like any working creative artist, it can take time to fall into until you experience a rush of imaginative stimulation.

You can stare at a blank canvas and be stumped for minutes, hours, and even days not knowing what to create. When this happens, communicate with your Spirit team to help. Get out of the way, do other things, and bam the connection is made. The Divine encouragement drops into one of your *clair* channels. This is the moment of discovery as the information is exceedingly crystal clear that you're stumped as to why you had not come to it prior.

Having writer's block is having a lack of inspiration.

This is why when my past love relationships have fallen apart, I've suddenly become uninspired and stopped creating. This state drives me crazy, but it's not something that can be switched on with the snap of a finger. There is a process I, or you, must go through to reach that place where your mind is clear again and able to create. In general, I pay attention to all that is around me. Not only because I pick up on every nuance that it becomes system overload, but I also look at the world noticing the people that pass me by. My ears perk up and pick up on dialogue and conversations between one another. Perhaps it's like eavesdropping, but if it's loud enough to hear, then I absorb that and write it down if it's poignant and relevant to what I'm seeking. My mind moves at a rapid pace and it is faster than my speech. This is my claircognizance channel. Somehow I have the ability to be alert to dialogue and everything around me. It's like the hyper watchfulness of a wild animal. When it's running at an optimum level, then I've risen into the creative zone before I max out.

Other ways to get inspired that work for me are by grounding yourself, getting into the great outdoors of nature, exercise, and watching what you ingest from foods and drinks. Pay attention to what foods you eat that cause you to feel lethargic afterwards. Get passionate about your life and all that is around you.

It is said that you cannot win the lottery if you do not buy a ticket. This is a metaphor that applies to everything in life. If you don't play, then you don't have a greater chance of winning. Use your creative spirit to your advantage.

The same way your life force is ignited, is the same

way that your creative spirit is unleashed. It's a lifestyle change you adopt by changing your attitude, feelings, and thoughts to that of optimism. It's finding a love and passion for something and diving into it. This is getting back into the joy of your life, which is an inspiration in itself. It is the beginning stages of pulling that tiny spark out of you that grows dim due to life circumstances. Light a match on this ember and allow it to inflame into creation. Escape into the magnificent worlds your mind daydreams and visualizes. Find something creative you enjoy doing and master it. Immerse your whole being into the revelations that come to you. Apply it to your daily life by coming up with new pioneering ways in excelling. This assists you in your soul's growth and raises your vibration to the place where the connection with Heaven is made. You are creatively powerful! Activate, awaken, and ignite this part of you. Experience the exhilarating high that comes with creativity.

Ignite Your Inner Life Force is an introduction guide for teens, young adults, and anyone seeking answers, messages, and guidance and surrounding spiritual empowerment. This is from understanding what Heaven, the soul, and spiritual beings are to knowing when you are connecting with your Spirit team of Guides and Angels.

Some of the topics covered are communicating with Heaven, working with your Spirit team, what your higher self is, your life purpose and soul contract, what the ego is, love and relationships, your vibration energy, shifting your consciousness and thinking for yourself even when you stand alone. This is an in-depth primer manual offering you foundation as you find a higher purpose navigating through your personal journey in today's modern day practical world.

Available in paperback and E-book
by Kevin Hunter,
REALM OF THE WISE ONE

In the Spirit Worlds and the dimensions that exist, reside numerous kingdoms that house a plethora of Spirits that inhabit various forms. One of these tribes is called the Wise Ones, a darker breed in the spirit realm who often chooses to incarnate into a human body one lifetime after another for important purposes.

The *Realm of the Wise One* takes you on a magical journey to the spirit world where the Wise Ones dwell. This is followed with in-depth and detailed information on how to recognize a human soul who has incarnated from the Wise One Realm.

Author, Kevin Hunter, is a Wise One who uses the knowledge passed onto him by his Spirit team of Guides and Angels to relay the wisdom surrounding all things Wise One. He discusses the traits, purposes, gifts, roles, and personalities among other things that make up someone who is a Wise One.

Wise Ones have come in the guises of teachers, shaman, leaders, hunters, mediums, entertainers and others. *Realm of the Wise One* is an informational guide devoted to the tribe of the Wise Ones, both in human form and on the other side.

Also available in
paperback and E-book
by Kevin Hunter,

REACHING FOR THE
WARRIOR WITHIN

Reaching for the Warrior Within is the author's personal story recounting a volatile childhood. This led him to a path of addictions, anxiety and overindulgence in alcohol, drugs, cigarettes and destructive relationships. As a survival mechanism, he split into many different "selves". He credits turning his life around, not by therapy, but by simultaneously paying attention to the messages he has been receiving from his Spirit team in Heaven since birth.

Kevin Hunter gains strength, healing and direction with the help of his own team of guides and angels. Living vicariously through this inspiring story will enable you to distinguish when you have been assisted on your own life path. *Reaching for the Warrior Within* attests that anyone can change if they pay attention to their own inner guidance system and take action. This can be from being a victim of child abuse, or a drug and alcohol user, to going after the jobs and relationships you want. This powerful story is for those seeking motivation to change, alter and empower their life one day at a time.

Available in paperback and E-book by Kevin Hunter,

TAROT CARD MEANINGS
*An Apprentice Guide of General Interpretations of an
Upright Tarot Card in a Reading for Love, Career, and
Other Matters*

Available in paperback and E-book by Kevin Hunter,

WARRIOR OF LIGHT
Messages from my Guides and Angels

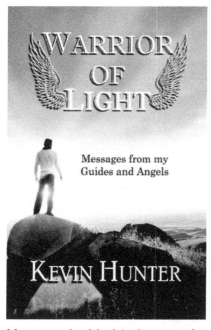

There are legions of angels, spirit guides, and departed loved ones in heaven that watch and guide you on your journey here on Earth. They are around to make your life easier and less stressful. Do you pay attention to the nudges, guidance, and messages given to you? There are many who live lives full of negativity and stress while trying to make ends meet. This can shake your faith as it leads you down paths of addictions, unhealthy life choices, and negative relationship connections. Learn how you can recognize the guidance of your own Spirit team of guides and angels around you.

Author, Kevin Hunter, relays heavenly guided messages about getting humanity, the world, and yourself into shape. He delivers the guidance passed onto him by his own Spirit team on how to fine tune your body, soul and raise your vibration. Doing this can help you gain hope and faith in your own life in order to start attracting in more abundance.

Available in paperback and E-book
by Kevin Hunter,

EMPOWERING SPIRIT WISDOM
A Warrior of Light's Guide on Love, Career and the Spirit World

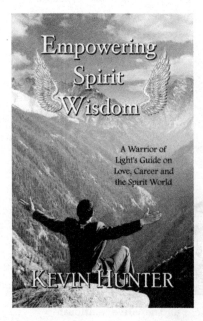

Kevin Hunter relays heavenly, guided messages for everyday life concerns with his book, *Empowering Spirit Wisdom*. Some of the topics covered are your soul, spirit and the power of the light, laws of attraction, finding meaningful work, transforming your professional and personal life, navigating through the various stages of dating and love relationships, as well as other practical affirmations and messages from the Archangels. Kevin Hunter passes on the sensible wisdom given to him by his own Spirit team in this inspirational book.

Available in paperback/E-book by Kevin Hunter,
DARKNESS OF EGO

The biggest cause of turmoil and conflict in one's life is executed by the human ego. All souls have an ego. The unruliest and destructive ego exists within every human soul. When the soul enters into a physical human body, the ego immediately compresses and then swells up. It is the higher self's goal to ensure that it remains in check while living an Earthly life.

The ego is what tests each soul along its journey. It is how one learns right from wrong. The experiences and challenges that the soul has while living in this Earthly life school contribute to the soul's growth. When a soul learns lessons, it is intended and expected to grow and enhance from the experience. Yet, there are a great many souls who do not learn lessons and remain in the same spot. The ill of the bunch wreaks all kinds of havoc, destruction, judgment and heart ache in its wake.

In *Darkness of Ego*, author Kevin Hunter infuses some of the guidance, messages, and wisdom he's received from his Spirit team surrounding all things ego related. The ego is one of the most damaging culprits in human life. Therefore, it is essential to understand the nature of the beast in order to navigate gracefully out of it when it spins out of control. Some of the topics covered in *Darkness of Ego* are humanity's destruction, mass hysteria, karmic debt, and the power of the mind, heaven's gate, the ego's war on love and relationships, and much more.

Available in paperback and E-book
by Kevin Hunter,
THE SEVEN DEADLY SINS

The Seven Deadly Sins is a mini-pocket book that takes a look at the traditional sins in a practical way. The Seven Deadly Sins in today's language would be the Seven Toxic Challenges. Being aware of these toxic challenges are helpful since falling into a deadly sin creates a block from achieving greatness, finding peace, and picking up on the messages and guidance coming in from Heaven. The messages and guidance are intended to help guide you along your path. You were born with an ego that expands as it enters the Earth's atmosphere. This ego causes you to struggle and have conflicts as it attempts to take over you and dominate your actions, thoughts, and feelings. When your ego runs recklessly it grows and expands into darkness. The dark ego is what prompts you to wrestle with challenges in this lifetime. These challenges were called *sin* during ancient times. The sins committed can delay you on your path and wreak havoc on your soul's innate system. This innate system is the higher self part of you that governs your life through a broader perspective.

The seven deadly sins were created in order to assist human souls in making sounder choices. They are challenges that all human souls wrestle with to one degree or another. When you're deeply absorbed in these toxic challenges, then it causes an array of issues and complications on your life path. These sins or challenges prevent the positive flow of energy and abundance in your life. They also play a hand at creating a block that stops up the communication line with your team on the Other Side. The sins or toxic challenges looked at include, Pride, Envy, Greed, Lust, Gluttony, Wrath and Sloth.

The *Warrior of Light* series of mini-pocket books are available in paperback and E-book by Kevin Hunter called, *Spirit Guides and Angels, Soul Mates and Twin Flames, Divine Messages for Humanity, Raising Your Vibration, Connecting with the Archangels*

About KEVIN HUNTER

Kevin Hunter is an author, love expert and channeler. His books tackle a variety of genres and tend to have a strong male protagonist. The messages and themes he weaves in his work surround Spirit's own communications of love and respect, which he channels and infuses into his writing and stories.

His books include the Warrior of Light series of books, *Warrior of Light: Messages from my Guides and Angels, Realm of the Wise One,* *Empowering Spirit Wisdom, Reaching for the Warrior Within, Darkness of Ego, Ignite Your Inner Life Force, Awaken Your Creative Spirit, Tarot Card Meanings,* and *The Seven Deadly Sins.* He is also the author of the singles dating love guide, *Love Party of One,* the horror, drama, *Paint the Silence,* and the modern day erotic love story, *Jagger's Revolution.*

Before writing books and stories, Kevin started out in the entertainment business in 1996 becoming actress Michelle Pfeiffer's personal development dude for her boutique production company, Via Rosa Productions. She dissolved her company after several years and he made a move into coordinating film productions for the big studios on such films as *One Fine Day, A Thousand Acres, The Deep End of the Ocean, Crazy in Alabama, Original Sin, The Perfect Storm, Harry Potter & the Sorcerer's Stone, Dr. Dolittle 2* and *Carolina.* He considers himself a love addict and beach bum born and raised in Los Angeles, California.

Visit www.kevin-hunter.com

Made in the USA
Monee, IL
06 December 2023

48377453R00115